Reading Abbey and the Abbey Quarter

Dr Peter Durrant MBE was County Archivist of Berkshire for 25 years until his retirement in 2014. He is a founder-member of the Berkshire Record Society and currently serves as the society's General Editor. He is Chairman of the Royal County of Berkshire Churches Trust, a Fellow of the Society of Antiquaries, and a past President of the Reading Branch of the Historical Association. He has been Chairman of the Friends of Reading Abbey since 2012.

John Painter retired from local government following 28 years working for Reading Borough Council. He has been actively involved with the Friends of Reading Abbey from 2011, and Secretary since 2013. His motive in joining the Friends of Reading Abbey was to support the council's efforts to consolidate the Abbey Ruins and get them re-opened to the public in plenty of time for 2021, the 900th anniversary of the Abbey's foundation.

Also published by Two Rivers Press

Reading Abbey
and the Abbey Quarter

Peter Durrant & John Painter | Friends of Reading Abbey

The Earley Charity

by hook or by crook

First published in the UK in 2018 by Two Rivers Press
7 Denmark Road, Reading RG1 5PA
www.tworiverspress.com

ISBN 978-1-909747-39-5

1 2 3 4 5 6 7 8 9

Two Rivers Press is represented in the UK by Inpress Ltd and distributed by NBNi.

Cover design by Nadja Guggi with a photograph by Chris Forsey
Text design by Nadja Guggi and typeset in Parisine

Printed and bound in Europe by Akcent Media

Contents

The decline and rediscovery of the Abbey Quarter | 59

Abbey Quarter Tour | 97

Acknowledgements

This book has been a pleasure to write. Reading Abbey and the Abbey Quarter are fascinating subjects in themselves, of continuing importance to the shape and development of Reading as a town, but in recent years they have not always been given the focused attention they deserve. We are delighted that the publication of this illustrated history and guide coincides with the completion of 'Reading Abbey Revealed', Reading Borough Council's £3.1m Heritage Lottery project to conserve the Abbey Ruins and Abbey gateway and to re-open both to the public for the future. It also anticipates the celebration of the 900th anniversary of the Abbey's foundation in 2021.

In writing this book, we are particularly grateful to the help we have received from our publishers, Two Rivers Press, who have been assiduous in keeping us to task and timetable; and to the Reading Abbey Revealed Project Team at Reading Museum (see page 117 for team members), who have commented on the text and provided access to pictures and illustrations held in the council collection. We are also grateful to Professor Brian Kemp (Emeritus of Reading University), John Mullaney, Dr Adrian Ailes, Professor Anne Curry and Adam Sowan for reading and commenting on the text. John Mullaney provided the text on the Abbey Ruins as a holy space in the 20th century and Barnaby Wheeler, Architect, Reading Hampshire Property Partnership, provided the text on conservation in the 21st century.

We must also thank the Friends of Reading Abbey (FORA) Committee for their support and encouragement. The Abbey Quarter Tour at the end of the book was developed from a leaflet guide originally written by Doug Beaumont, a committee member, and published by FORA. The authors of this book are, respectively, the Chairman and Secretary of the Friends of Reading Abbey, and one of our objectives was to publish a book that is accessible to local readers, both in content and price. On price, FORA have provided financial support to help keep the purchase cost down. The Earley Charity have also made a grant to the publishers. As a result of these two acts of generosity, and of help in kind from the Reading Abbey Revealed Project Team at Reading Museum, we are able to make the illustrated guide available for purchase at £9.99.

The book is dedicated to the memory of Dr Julia Boorman and Sabina Sutherland. Julia was actively involved in the Friends from their formation until her untimely death from cancer in 2012, when she was our Chairman. Sabina was also a long-standing member of the Friends who died from cancer, before her time, in 2014 and whose generous legacy bequest to FORA has been used to fund this publication.

PD & JGP
June 2018

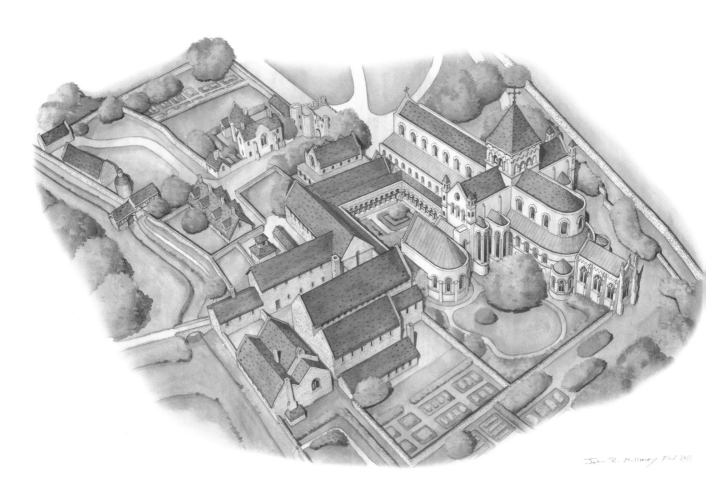

INTRODUCING
THE ABBEY STORY

An overview of the history of the Abbey

Henry I depicted in a window
in St James's church.

Opposite page:
A model of Reading Abbey on display
in Reading Museum.

Reading Abbey was founded in 1121 by Henry I – son of William the Conqueror – to be his place of burial. A royal abbey from its inception, it remained under royal patronage until its dissolution by Henry VIII in 1539. At that point it was one of the ten wealthiest monastic foundations in England, with a mitred abbot who sat in Parliament.

It is a challenge today to imagine the view from the rivers Thames and Kennet of the enormous Abbey church, faced in honey-coloured stone, glinting in the sun as it towered over and dominated the market town of Reading. In line with its royal foundation, its size, structure and architecture were on a lavish and elaborate scale. Its nave, at 200 ft (61 m) long, exceeded that of Durham Cathedral, and the church was faced in the Taynton stone that was later used for Blenheim Palace. Reading Abbey was predominantly a Romanesque building, completed in a new hybrid Anglo-Norman style in 1164, with a Gothic lady chapel added subsequently at its east end (1314). It had a significant impact on the social, economic and spatial development of the town which is still evident in the street pattern of the town centre, and in particular in the area now known as the Abbey Quarter.

Reading was one of the leading Benedictine abbeys in Europe. Throughout its 400-year life the royal abbey was visited regularly by the king and his court and hosted parliaments, royal weddings and other historic events. It was strategically placed on major communication routes that linked London and Windsor to the south and west of England, and the fact that it possessed, from early days, the hand of St James the Great and other important relics connected it into the continental pilgrimage routes leading to Santiago de Compostela. Though much reduced since its days of glory, it is still the town's pre-eminent historic monument.

The last abbot, Hugh Cook Faringdon, refused to surrender the Abbey as part of the Dissolution of the larger monastic houses demanded by Henry VIII and was executed in the Forbury for treason in November 1539. The Abbey was dissolved, passed into the hands of the crown, and the monastic buildings were converted into a royal palace.

The Abbey church was broken up from 1548 onwards. The site suffered further damage during the English Civil War, when it was part of the defences of Reading. But some of the buildings and grounds remained in use: in particular the dormitory of the hospitium, which was shared by the corporation of Reading and Reading School; the inner Abbey gateway; and the Forbury, the open space in the public part of the Abbey precinct which had been, and continued to be, the place where fairs were held. Parts of the church and monastic buildings also survive in a ruined state, including the transepts, the chapter house, dormitory and south refectory wall, and the Abbey mill arch.

In the 18th century, the Abbey was increasingly appreciated as a picturesque ruin. Since the late 18th century, the Abbey Quarter has been the focus of civic and other public redevelopment; it attracted significant architectural contributions from Alfred Waterhouse (Reading Town Hall), Augustus Pugin (St James's church) and Sir George Gilbert Scott (Reading Gaol, Abbey gateway restoration). During the 19th century, the Forbury and the Abbey Ruins were consolidated as public open space and taken over by the Borough as a major civic amenity. Despite threats and challenges during the 20th century, this they remain, and in the first two decades of the 21st century, both have benefited from Heritage Lottery funding.

Archaeological surveys and descriptions

General Plan of the Ruins of Reading Abbey, Surveyed by Sir Henry Englefield, Feb 1779. Drawing (possibly a print) showing the layout of Reading Abbey with two small details of walls.

Opposite page:
Dr Hurry produced many works about the Abbey including these detailed plans showing both the standing ruins and the supposed footprint of the Abbey buildings, including the church.

The Abbey site was surveyed in 1650, when it had passed into parliamentary jurisdiction. The first and only mapped survey of the Abbey site was by Sir Henry Englefield, published in 1779. Subsequent plans of the area by Coates (1802), Man (1813/1816) and Buckler (1823–24) were based on Englefield's original. The Reading architect F.W. Albury conducted an unpublished survey of the area in 1879 that was the subject of a report to the Berkshire Archaeological Society in 1881. Dr Jamieson Hurry, a local medical man, published his definitive work *Reading Abbey* in 1900. Cecil Slade, from the University of Reading, excavated the north-eastern parts of the chancel and ambulatory of the Abbey church under the prison car park between 1970 and 1973. There have been other subsequent excavations of parts of the southern half of the precinct around Abbey Street and Abbey Square as they have been developed since the 1990s.

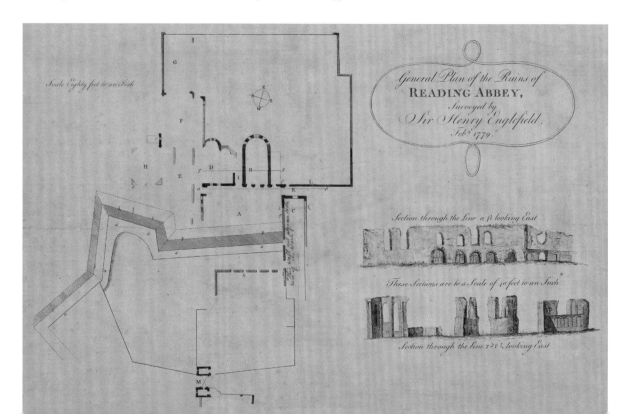

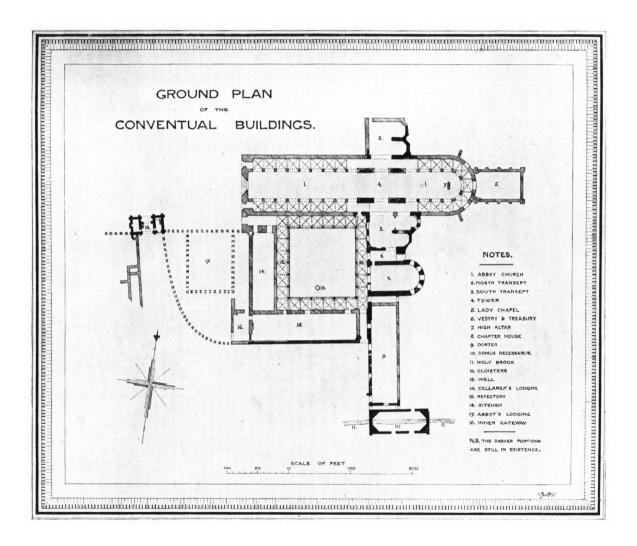

GROUND PLAN
OF THE
CONVENTUAL BUILDINGS.

NOTES.

1. ABBEY CHURCH
2. NORTH TRANSEPT
3. SOUTH TRANSEPT
4. TOWER
5. LADY CHAPEL
6. VESTRY & TREASURY
7. HIGH ALTAR
8. CHAPTER HOUSE
9. DORTER
10. DOMUS NECESSARIÆ
11. HOLY BROOK
12. CLOISTERS
13. WELL
14. CELLARER'S LODGING
15. REFECTORY
16. KITCHEN
17. ABBOT'S LODGING
18. INNER GATEWAY

N.B. THE DARKER PORTIONS
ARE STILL IN EXISTENCE.

SCALE OF FEET

100   50.   0   100   200

Henry I

Henry I (bottom left) holding Reading Abbey, in *Historia Anglorum* by Matthew Paris, *c.* 1250.

Opposite page:
A bearded Henry I.
Linocut by Sally Castle, 2017

The restored Henry I memorial plaque.

Henry I (1068–1135) was the fourth and youngest son of William I (the Conqueror) and Matilda of Flanders. He succeeded his brother William II (Rufus) as king of England in 1100, following Rufus's death in a hunting accident in the New Forest. He was Duke of Normandy from 1106 following his defeat of his eldest brother Robert in battle. He was educated in Latin and known as Beauclerc. He was a harsh but effective ruler who strengthened the Anglo-Saxon systems of government by establishing the royal exchequer and itinerant justices.

He married Matilda of Scotland in 1100, a great-granddaughter of the Saxon king Edmund Ironside, thereby uniting the Norman and Saxon royal lines. Queen Matilda died in 1118. They had two children – a son and heir, William, and a daughter, Matilda, who was married when young to the Holy Roman Emperor. William died in the wreck of the White Ship, off Barfleur, Normandy, in 1120, leaving Henry without a direct male successor. In 1121 Henry married Adeliza of Louvain, but they had no children.

Henry founded Reading Abbey within a year of William's death. It was very richly endowed from the start and constructed to a high standard of craftsmanship and materials. King Henry, Queen Adeliza and the Empress Matilda all made substantial grants of land to the Abbey. Henry died near Rouen, in Normandy, on 1 December 1135, and his body was brought back for burial in his Abbey in Reading, as he had specified. He was interred on 5 January 1136. Following his death, Henry was succeeded not by his daughter, the Empress Matilda, but by his nephew, Stephen. There then followed the period of civil war known as The Anarchy, when it was said that Christ and his saints slept.

Henry is often shown to be heavily bearded. In 1105, the French Bishop Serlo of Sées preached a sermon in Henry's presence which compared bearded men to 'goats and Saracens'. The Anglo-Norman monk and chronicler Orderic Vitalis also railed against the King's beard. In the face of such clerical opposition, Henry was eventually induced to shave. This may be reflected in different images of the king. The painting by Matthew Paris above, from

*c.*1250, shows a clean-shaven king holding his Abbey. Later coinage showed Henry with a small beard.

A memorial to Henry I was first installed on the wall facing the ruins of the south transept, on 18 June 1921 as part of the 800th anniversary of the foundation the Abbey. However, the original plaque sustained severe water damage and the lead lettering was beyond repair, so it was expertly recreated by conservation specialists Cliveden Conservation in time for the re-opening of the Abbey site on 16 June 2018. Despite the severe erosion, they managed to retain the original bronze crown which has been reinstated as it was on the original plaque and a protective stone shelf has been installed to prevent future water damage.

The outline of the Abbey overlaid on an OS map of 1879–1902. The river Kennet can be seen to the south of the Abbey. The Thames runs just north of the map's boundary.

Cholsey Barn. The sheer size of this tithe barn indicates how wealthy Reading Abbey was.

Thomas Becket stained glass window in St James's church, Reading.

Foundation

The Abbey was founded in 1121, and the monastic buildings were completed within five years. King Henry I's foundation charter of 1125 gave the monks a generous endowment of lands, churches and privileges. The Abbey church took over 40 years to build, but the choir was sufficiently advanced at the time of his burial in 1136 to permit King Henry I to be buried in front of the high altar. The church was dedicated by Thomas Becket, Archbishop of Canterbury, on 19 April 1164, in the presence of King Henry II.

According to the foundation charter, the Abbey was built for the salvation of the king's soul and those of his dead relatives: his father (William I), mother (Matilda of Flanders), brother (William II), first wife and queen (Matilda), and his recently-drowned son and sole male heir, William. The Abbey was intended as a family memorial and Henry's burial place. The monks said prayers for the king's soul daily until the Dissolution over 400 years later.

The Abbey was founded on land owned by the king on a gravel ridge between the river Thames and the river Kennet, to the east of the Saxon settlement of Reading which was at that time centred on St Mary's church and what is now St Mary's Butts. Henry I's reasons for choosing Reading are not known, but are likely to have been informed by the combination of the strategic geographic location and royal ownership of a site that was most probably unoccupied at this time. We know from the records of Henry's itineraries that he visited Reading on several occasions between 1100 and 1120.

The foundation charter and later endowments gave the Abbey extensive lands in Berkshire and other counties as far afield as Kent and the Midlands. A dependent priory was founded at Leominster in Herefordshire, and the Abbey also supported another priory on the Isle of May in the Firth of Forth until the 14th century. The Abbey held the manor of Cholsey (now Oxfordshire), where it had a great tithe barn that was 300ft (91m) long. The endowment also included lands in west Reading which Henry I's father, William the Conqueror, had given, 50 years earlier, to the abbey he had established at the site of the Battle of Hastings. This part of Reading is still known as Battle, despite the connection having been severed 900 years ago.

LIFE IN THE ABBEY

Abbots and monks

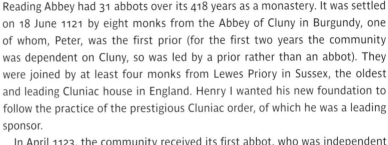

Opposite page:
Election of the Mayor of Reading by Abbot Thorne in 1460, oil on canvas, by Stephen Reid, 1921. This painting from the 20th century shows the abbot wearing the episcopal mitre, ring, dalmatic, tunic and sandals.

This memorial to Hugh of Amiens can be seen today in the remains of the chapter house.

Reading Abbey had 31 abbots over its 418 years as a monastery. It was settled on 18 June 1121 by eight monks from the Abbey of Cluny in Burgundy, one of whom, Peter, was the first prior (for the first two years the community was dependent on Cluny, so was led by a prior rather than an abbot). They were joined by at least four monks from Lewes Priory in Sussex, the oldest and leading Cluniac house in England. Henry I wanted his new foundation to follow the practice of the prestigious Cluniac order, of which he was a leading sponsor.

In April 1123, the community received its first abbot, who was independent of Cluny. He was Hugh of Amiens, who had been the Prior of Lewes and therefore of the Cluniac Order. Abbot Hugh ruled until 1130, when he was succeeded by Abbot Anscher who, like Hugh, had been Prior of Lewes. The eighth abbot, Hugh II (1186–99), had also been Prior of Lewes, and later moved from Reading to become Abbot of Cluny.

In 1191, Pope Clement III granted the Abbot the right to wear the episcopal mitre, ring, gloves, dalmatic, tunic and sandals. This was an honour granted only to the great English Benedictine houses such as Westminster and St Albans. In the later Middle Ages, Reading was recognised as a leading English Benedictine monastery.

The later abbots of Reading attended Parliament as spiritual peers. They were Lords of the Manor of Reading and had local administrative functions. They also acted as collectors of papal taxation in the diocese of Salisbury, in which Reading was located until the 19th century.

The Abbey was founded with the intention to accommodate 100 monks. By the mid-15th century, following the Black Death, the number had fallen, with 34 (of whom 31 were ordained priests) recorded in 1446 as taking part in the election of the new abbot. We do not know the number at the Dissolution in 1539, but 15 years later, in the reign of Mary I, pensions were still being paid to 13 former monks.

13

Life in the Abbey was dominated by the daily rounds of worship and prayer in the Abbey church: the *Opus Dei* or work of God. Monks attended eight services a day, beginning with matins before dawn and finishing with compline at around 9pm before they retired to bed. Mass was said daily, usually in the morning. Each service had its own liturgy, sung to plainchant, and included psalms, readings from the Bible, and prayers. Prayers for the souls of the departed were said regularly on the anniversary of their death. Services could be attended with elaborate ceremonial, especially on feasts and anniversaries. A late 13th-century manuscript lists several major feasts, including the Annunciation, Easter, Pentecost, St James's Day and Christmas, and a still larger number of lesser feasts, including commemoration of past abbots.

A very significant anniversary was that of the death of the founder, Henry I, which began on the evening before and lasted the whole of the day itself. It involved an elaborate and colourful ceremony: the church was adorned with the finest hangings, the abbot and senior monks wore rich vestments, candles were placed around the king's tomb, which was wreathed with incense, the Abbey bells were rung and every priest present celebrated mass. On such feast days more generous meals were provided for the community.

Meals were eaten in the refectory, in silence, while one monk read from the Bible or the life of a saint. Except on feast days, they were usually modest, comprising mainly bread and vegetables, with some eggs, cheese and fish.

When not in the church or the refectory, monks would spend most of their time in or around the cloister. We know that the Abbey had a substantial library, amounting as early as the end of the 12th century to nearly 300 volumes, and we can imagine many of the monks reading or writing, as for the greater part of the Abbey's existence all books were written by hand, and many were elaborately decorated. However, not all monks worked in this way. Others with particular skills might assist with or superintend the maintenance of the buildings or the gardens or be engaged with some of the many administrative tasks involved in running a large organisation.

While the abbot or, in his absence, the prior, had overall responsibility for the running of the Abbey, other senior monks had charge of discrete areas, such as the sacrist (responsible for the fabric), the hospitaller (responsible for looking after pilgrims and visitors), the cellarer (responsible for supplies of

Hugh Faringdon (Abbot Cook) and his crest, stained glass window in St James's church, Reading.

Opposite page:
Monks reading a book.

The cellarer of the abbey was responsible for supplies of food and drink.

food and drink), the almoner (responsible for the distribution of relief to the poor) and the treasurer (responsible for the Abbey's treasures and money).

The work of the Abbey was supported by many servants. Some of these were professional men, since the Abbey needed a steward to manage its estate and a lawyer to deal with legal and property matters. Others, most of whom came in from the town each day, helped in the kitchens or gardens, in the mill, the bakehouse and the stables, while carpenters and masons were employed in practical jobs around the site. The abbot himself had a large number of personal servants, sometimes as many as 40, as befitted the head of a major abbey and a man who had a seat in the House of Lords and the status equivalent to that of a bishop.

Pilgrims, relics and miracles

Pilgrimage was important in the Middle Ages. In spite of the difficulties involved, people were prepared to travel great distances to favoured shrines. The Holy Land, Rome and Compostela were the chief centres internationally, but greater and lesser abbeys and priories across Europe attracted large numbers of pilgrims. Reading was prominent among them. The importance of pilgrimage to Reading may be gauged from the fact that the hospitium, which provided accommodation for pilgrims, was built to a generous scale, with one estimate that it could hold 400 guests at a time.

Chaucer's *Canterbury Tales* may suggest that one reason to go on a pilgrimage was to have a good time, but there were more serious reasons too. Chief among them were a penance for past sins, to gain an indulgence (a reduction of time spent in purgatory after death and before entering heaven) and to seek a cure for illness or disease. Relics of apostles and saints were believed to have special powers of healing, and devotion at a saint's shrine was a common way of seeking relief.

Relics were housed in caskets known as reliquaries. Made of gold and silver and often adorned with jewels, these were objects of great richness and beauty that helped to emphasise the value of the relic they contained. Because of their importance, relics would usually have been locked away in the abbey treasury and brought out to be shown in the church only for special occasions, such as the saint's feast day, when pilgrims would file round the church, pausing before the relics to make their devotions, light a candle and leave a gift.

Reading was an attractive place of pilgrimage because of the quality of its relics. Already by the late 12th century the Abbey had well over 200, including fragments of the True Cross and items associated with Christ himself, with the Blessed Virgin, and with numerous apostles and martyrs. Chief among them was the hand of St James the Great. Presented to the Abbey by its founder, Henry I, at the request of his daughter, the Empress Matilda (who had brought the hand – part of the imperial crown jewels – to England in 1126 after the death of her husband, the Holy Roman Emperor Henry V), this was at the time the pre-eminent relic of an apostle in the kingdom, and it rapidly became

It is unlikely that this really is the hand of St James but this relic may still be seen in St Peter's Church in Marlow.

Opposite page:
The Abbey's emblem may be seen incorporated into the Victoria Gates to Forbury Gardens.

The head of a pilgrim to Santiago de Compostela wearing a carved scallop shell, carved on the Abbey Gateway.

credited with miraculous powers. A fascinating manuscript of the late 12th century describes in great and colourful detail some 28 miracles attributed to it: a woman from Earley was cured of dropsy; John the Clerk had his speech restored; Edward Haver of Reading was cured of a tumour, as was Thomas the monk; Alice, a girl from Essex, had her withered arm restored to strength, as did Ysembela, a girl from Seaford in Sussex, while a girl from Suffolk who appeared to have no bones in her legs had them wonderfully restored; a woman from Collingbourne Ducis in Wiltshire was cured of a wasting disease, and a woman from Curridge, near Newbury, was cured of epilepsy; and Osbert, Prior of Notley Abbey in Buckinghamshire, who suffered from a 'most grievous affliction of the eyes', which caused him 'intense pain and ... acute torment', found the pain banished and his sight restored.

The link between Reading Abbey and St James, who was believed to have been buried at Santiago de Compostela in Spain, was reflected in the Abbey's emblem, which consisted of three scallop shells, the tokens traditionally given to pilgrims completing the Compostela pilgrimage.

At the Dissolution, the Abbey's relics were itemised by Dr John London, the royal agent responsible for the suppression of monasteries in Berkshire and Oxfordshire, during a visit in 1538, after which he locked them up behind the high altar and kept the key. From here they were most probably taken to London to be destroyed. The Abbey's library, plate and other treasures were dispersed or destroyed. However, a relic once claimed to be the hand of St James is held by the Catholic church of St Peter in Marlow: a withered left hand found in a wall at the east end of the Abbey church by workmen digging foundations for the new gaol in 1786.

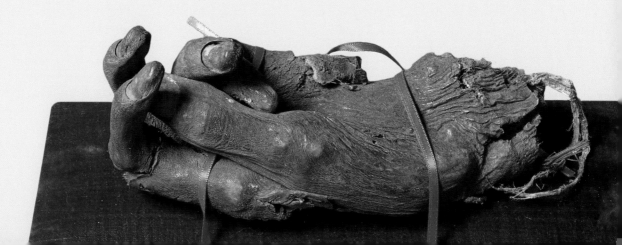

Economy

Opposite page:
Map of Reading included in
John Speed's *The Theatre of Empire
of Great Britaine*, 1610–11 (confusingly
included in the county map of
Buckinghamshire). The map shows
the influence of the Abbey on the
town's road layout.

The Abbey had extensive landholdings, particularly in Berkshire and neighbouring counties, which helped to fund its operation. At the time of the Dissolution the Abbey's income was valued at just under £2000 a year, putting it in the top ten wealthiest monastic establishments in England.

The abbot was Lord of the Manor and Hundred of Reading, and was also Lord of the Hundreds of Leominster (Herefordshire) and Hoo (Kent). The Abbey was free from some taxation and the monks were not liable to tolls on rivers, roads or markets across the country. The abbot had extensive judicial privileges, a manor court and a gaol.

The Abbey had a mill on the Holy Brook, a channel of the River Kennet that still runs through the centre of Reading. The mill has been demolished, though a double arch over the Holy Brook remains. The mill served the needs of the Abbey and would also (for a charge) have ground corn for the people of Reading and its neighbourhood.

The Abbey also established its own market in the triangular site now known as Market Place, the town market until the 1970s when it was moved to near St Mary's Butts. To encourage (or divert) trade, the Abbey developed a new approach route to the Market Place from Whitley Street in the south to capture traffic from London and Southampton: this is the route followed by Silver Street, London Street and Duke Street (as against the older route of Southampton Street and Bridge Street). During the Middle Ages, linking roads were developed between St Mary's Butts and the Market Place and Abbey, in particular Minster Street and Broad Street, with Friar Street (originally New Street) developing later to the north. Thus the road network of Reading town centre was established, and it is still very recognisable to local residents today.

The Abbey had the right to hold three fairs a year which probably took place in the Forbury, the public space within the enclosed Abbey precinct. Between 1129 and 1133, Henry I granted the Abbey the privilege of a fair of St Laurence (10–13 August); Henry II in 1164 added a second fair on the feast of St James the Great (25–28 July); and King John granted a third, on the feast of St Philip and St James the Less in 1205 (30 April –3 May).

Initially the Abbey had a right to have a mint in Reading to produce coins, but this had fallen out of use by the time of the reign of Henry II.

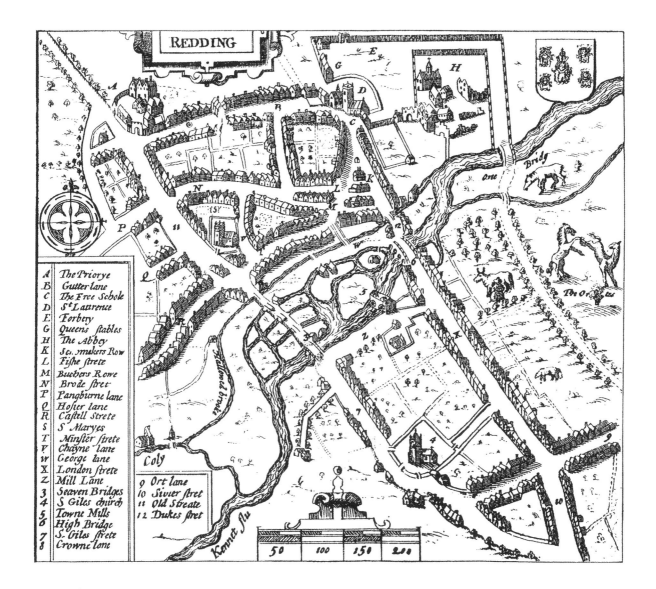

REDDING

A	The Priorye
B	Gutter lane
C	The Free Schole
D	S.t Lawrence
E	Forbey
G	Queens stables
H	The Abbey
K	Sc. makers Row
L	Fishe strete
M	Buchers Rowe
N	Brode stret
P	Pangburne lane
Q	Hosier lane
R	Castell Strete
S	S. Maryes
T	Minster strete
V	Chayne lane
W	George lane
X	London strete
Z	Mill Lane
3	Seaven Bridges
4	S. Giles church
5	Towne Mills
6	High Bridge
7	S. Giles strete
8	Crowne lone

9	Ort lane
10	Sivier stret
11	Old Streate
12	Dukes stret

Coly

Kennet flu

50 100 150 200

The Orte

Orte

Bridg

Relations with the town

The 1254 agreement made between the Abbey and the town following the 1253 charter granted by the king.

In part because of its economic and judicial roles, the relationship between the Abbey and the town was not always harmonious. The abbot owned the town's fisheries, mills and market. He also controlled the town guild, appointing the warden, controlling admission to the merchant guild and requiring guildsmen to pay an annual market tax (*Chepyn gavel*). The guild sought to challenge this predominance and strike out for independence in 1253, during the reign of Henry III, when they assaulted the abbot's bailiffs and ended up in court. The king restored peace by upholding the supreme authority of the abbot, but also granting the guild a Charter, the first charter in favour of Reading's townspeople. Disputation continued into 1254 when a separate concord recognised the guild's right to hold its own market and have a guild hall (eventually established in Yield Hall Lane, now part of The Oracle development), and the guild in return recognised the abbot's right to appoint one of their number each year as Chief Warden (mayor) (see the picture on page 12).

Disputes continued during the 14th and 15th centuries. In the latter, Henry VI gave permission to the mayor to have a mace carried before him, and one was bought in 1459, only for the right to be withdrawn shortly afterwards. From 1480, the *Chepyn gavel* payment passed to the guild. In 1487 a charter of Henry VII recognised the mayor and gave to the guild the right to elect two sergeants-at-arms. The abbot, however, refused to appoint the mayor for four years. The struggle again ended in the courts, which ruled in favour of the abbot in 1507. Thus the Abbey entered the 16th century with the abbot still in dispute with the town about municipal privileges and still nominally in control.

calli remaneat ⁊ Expliciunt statuta. ⁊ Et incipit final' concord'.

H̅ec est final' acordia facta in curia dn̅i reg' apd̅ Westm̅. In an̅no Ꝑtificacionis lib. q̅ nie. anno. R. reg'. henr̅ic. fil' reg' Johis. Tricesimo octauo. coram henrico de Bacon. henr̅ de la mar. henr̅ de Maurtcon. Nicholao de turri. Iustic̅. Radulfo fil' Richi de Certmod. ⁊ aluel te senescall'. Et alijs dn̅i fidelib; ⁊ ibi ꝑsentib; int̅ henr̅ wille. ⁊ ca= titele. de W̅lueseye. ⁊ senescall'. Gildr̅ de Radinḡ. Et Burgens̅ eide ville quer̅. Et Rich̅ abbem de Radinḡ de foro. de consuetud. ⁊ seruic̅ que Idem abbas exigebat de ꝑdc̅is Burgensib; Vnde idem Burgentes q̅ti fuer̅t q̅d ꝑdc̅s abbas distruxit eos ad placitand' alibi q̅m in Gilda sua com̅u. Et q̅d abstulit ab eis Gildam suam m̅cand' cu̅ ꝑudens. Et ꝑterea q̅d ꝑdc̅t' abbas amouit m̅catum ville de Radinḡ a loco q̅ antiq̅² tener̅ sol̅. Et ꝑterea q̅d exigebat ab eisd̅ Burgensib; alia q̅ suetudines. ⁊ alia seruicia q̅m face debuer̅t. ⁊ face c̅suer̅t. temporib; ꝑdecessorum ꝑdci dn̅i reg' regni angl'. Q̅s c̅suetudines. ⁊ que seruicia da̅ Burgens̅ eide abb̅i no̅ cognouerunt. ⁊ vnde sut int̅ eos i cade curia. scilicet q̅d ꝑdes abbas c̅cessit ꝑ se. ⁊ successorib; suis. ⁊ ecc̅ sua de Radinḡ. ꝑdc̅m Burgensib; ⁊ eoꝝ hedib; q̅d m̅catum bladi. Tuella de Radinḡ sit in loco illo inꝑpetuu̅. Vbi ꝑus c̅ solebat. et q̅d omia alia vendit̅ in locum illu̅ inquib; vendi ꝑus c̅suer̅t. ⁊ q̅d ꝑ ꝉ̅ u̅ ꝉ̅ gildhallam m̅cand' in villa de Radinḡ cu̅

THE ROYAL CONNECTION

Opposite page:
Marriage of John of Gaunt and Blanche
of Lancaster at Reading Abbey in 1359,
oil on canvas by Horace Boardman Wright,
1914

Royal visitors

Opposite page:
Edward IV and Elizabeth Woodville at
Reading Abbey in 1464, oil on canvas
by Ernest Board, 1923

Reading was founded as a royal abbey, and as such had a regular place in the itinerary of visits by king and court throughout the Middle Ages. Crowned kings from Henry II to Henry VIII often stayed for major church feasts or held council meetings at Reading during their reigns.

Henry I (1100–1135) granted the foundation charter to the Abbey and, at his request, was buried there. His widow, Queen Adeliza, visited the Abbey on the first anniversary of the king's death, in December 1136, when she made a generous endowment to provide for the annual celebration of the date in perpetuity.

Stephen (1135–54) was present at King Henry's funeral. He visited the Abbey in 1140 on his way to Wallingford. The Empress Matilda was received in Reading with great honour in 1141, after the defeat and capture of Stephen at the Battle of Lincoln, when she issued five charters in favour of the Abbey. These included confirmation of grants previously made by her father and Queen Adeliza. Stephen later founded his own abbey, in Faversham, on the same Cluniac model as Reading.

Henry II (1154–89) is recorded as staying at Reading on ten occasions, including that of the trial by combat between Henry of Essex and Robert de Montfort held on Fry's Island in the River Thames in 1163, the hallowing of the completed new Abbey (1164) and the visit to England of Heraclius, Patriarch of Jerusalem, in 1185.

Richard I (1189–99) held a Great Council at the Abbey in 1191. In 1189 he had required the surrender of the silver reliquary that had contained the hand of St James to help fund his participation in the Third Crusade.

King John (1199–1216), Richard's brother, visited Reading on 22 occasions and stayed for a total of 61 days during his 17-year reign. He was a generous benefactor to the Abbey and, in 1192, before his accession, had made an annual gift of alms to the Abbey that funded the provision of a new reliquary for the hand of St James in compensation for that surrendered to his brother.

John's son, Henry III (1216–72) visited Reading on a regular basis on his journeys from Westminster and Windsor to Winchester, Clarendon (Salisbury)

and Marlborough, or to Wallingford and Woodstock. He stayed at the Abbey for a total of 238 days, including Easter on six occasions and Christmas and Whitsun on one occasion each.

Kings Edward I and II were less frequent visitors. Edward III (1327–77) was more enthusiastic, visiting 15 times (30 days) up to 1345. During his reign four royal weddings took place in the Abbey. The first was in September 1342, when the king's second surviving son, Lionel of Antwerp, Duke of Clarence, married Elizabeth de Burgh. The other three were in 1359: on 19 May John of Gaunt, the king's third surviving son, married Blanche, the heiress of the Duke of Lancaster, through whom John then became Duke; also in May, the king's 12-year old daughter, Margaret, married John Earl of Pembroke; and the king's three-year-old granddaughter, Philippa of Clarence, was betrothed to Edmund Mortimer, later Earl of March.

Opposite page:

Parliament of Henry VI at Reading Abbey in 1453, oil on canvas by Stephen Reid, 1920

During his reign, Richard II (1377–99) also visited up to 12 times, for a total of 46 days, including a long stay in 1389, when a council was held where the king declared himself of an age to rule. Richard also ordered the Abbey to restore, during his reign, the monument to Henry I on his tomb.

Royal visits during the 15th century were less frequent. King Henry IV (1139–1413) stayed only once, in 1403, on the journey to Winchester for his wedding to his second wife, Joan of Navarre. Henry V visited at least once, in 1417, when he held a council to raise money for his 1417 campaign to France.

Henry VI (1422–61, 1470–71) visited seven times, staying for a total of 88 days. This included the only parliament specifically convened at Reading Abbey, in 1453, which was held in the Abbey refectory. The parliament of November 1439 adjourned to Reading in January 1440 to escape the plague in London.

Henry's replacement as king, Edward IV (1461–70, 1471–83), visited Reading twice, for a council in 1464 and an adjourned parliament in 1467. It was during the former that Edward presented Elizabeth Woodville, whom he had married secretly earlier in the year, to the council as his wife and queen.

Richard III (1483–85) visited Reading for two days in late July 1483 as part of his post-coronation progress through the country from London to York via Oxford.

Henry VII (1485–1509) is recorded as staying at Reading on three occasions during his reign; he was possibly also present in 1486 when he founded the grammar school in the hospitium building. His son Arthur, Prince of Wales, was at Reading in 1501, while waiting to meet his new bride, Catherine of Aragon, as she progressed from Plymouth to London for their wedding.

Henry VIII (1509–1547) visited Reading regularly, primarily for hunting in the abbot's deer park (Whitley), including in the summer of 1509 and most summers thereafter. This arrangement continued after the Dissolution. The king visited Reading Abbey in 1520, two days after the installation of Hugh Cook Faringdon as abbot, from whom the king received a generous gift of fish. Henry brought Anne Boleyn to Reading in 1529 and again, as queen, in 1535.

Royal burials

Opposite page:
Burial of King Henry I at Reading
Abbey in January 1136. Oil on canvas
by Harry Morley, 1916

King Henry I founded Reading Abbey, and at his request he was buried in front of the high altar, on 5 January 1136.

Henry's second wife and queen, Adeliza of Louvain, was buried in Reading Abbey in 1151. Following Henry's death, Adeliza had re-married and was therefore not buried with Henry, but to the right side of the king's tomb.

Reading Abbey did not become a major royal necropolis. However, some burials of royal children did take place at the Abbey, as follows:

- William of Poitiers (1156), eldest son and heir presumptive of Henry II, who died aged three at Wallingford Castle

- Reginald de Dunstanville, Earl of Cornwall (1175) – one of Henry I's many illegitimate children – died aged 65, buried to the right of the king in the high choir.

- John (1233) and Isabella (1234), the first two infant children of Richard of Cornwall, Henry III's younger brother

- Constance of York (1416), daughter of Edmund Duke of York, Edward III's fourth surviving son, who died aged 42 and was the last royal burial at the Abbey.

THE ABBEY BUILDINGS

The gatehouse and outer court

The Abbey gateway and St Nicolas Church in Abingdon. The outer gateway and St Laurence's church in Reading would have had a very similar appearance.

Opposite page:
This digital 3D reconstruction of the Abbey precinct shows the gatehouse at the far end by St Laurence's church, and the outer court.

If, around the year 1500, you had stood at the north end of Reading's market place, next to St Laurence's church, and looked east along what is now The Forbury, a very different sight from today's would have met your eyes. Instead of the road between the church and the buildings opposite, you would have been confronted by an enormous two-storey gatehouse, the compter gate. This was one of five gatehouses in the Abbey (the only one remaining is the inner Abbey gateway, giving access to the monastic quarters), and it was the entrance through which most visitors would have passed. This gatehouse was a substantial building, designed to impress. Besides the great arched gateway itself, it accommodated a porter's lodge comprising cellar, hall, buttery, three chambers and three garrets. The first floor may have been the abbot's prison (compter).

Once through the gate, you would have stood in the outer, public, court of the Abbey. To the right, leading towards the inner Abbey gateway, was a wall that divided the public area from the monastic quarters. To the left stood the east end of St Laurence's church and beyond that was the hospitium or Abbey guest house, part of which still stands. There was no churchyard at St Laurence's at that time: burials took place to the north of the Abbey church. The rest of the area, covering today's Forbury Gardens, was open space. But what would have struck you most, some 650 ft (200 m) ahead, was the great west front of the Abbey church.

The church

Peterborough Cathedral

Opposite page:
The remains of the founder's
chapel, off the south transept.

The Abbey church, dedicated to the Virgin Mary and St John, was one of the greatest Romanesque churches of medieval England. Built between 1121 and 1164, it matched in scale and magnificence the great cathedrals of Peterborough and Ely that still survive today. According to the architect Frederick Albury, who surveyed the site in the 1870s, the whole church was 450 ft (138 m) in length. The nave alone measured 200 ft (61 m) – longer than the nave of Westminster Abbey (166 ft/50 m). The nave and chancel measured 95 ft (29 m) in width; and the transepts stretched some 200 ft (61 m) from end to end. Its height cannot be known with certainty, but the walls to the eaves were probably more than twice the height of the highest standing remains (in the south transept).

The church was Romanesque in style and cruciform in plan. In this regard it followed the standard layout for a major church building of the period but was much larger in size and grander in decoration. Some reconstructions show flanking towers on the west front, but this is not proven by archaeology: the west front probably matched the shape of the nave and aisles, with a tall central gable and lower roofs on either side. It is likely that the aisles were surmounted by a gallery, as at Peterborough and elsewhere, but this is conjectural.

The nave was probably divided into ten bays with round arches supported by cylindrical columns. At the crossing, massive piers supported the great weight of the tower: parts of the south-east and south-west piers can still be seen. Each of the transepts, to the north and south of the crossing, had two chapels, of which those in the south transept remain (see p. 34).

Beyond the crossing stretched the chancel, four bays long and with an apsidal (semi-circular) east end. Here, in the original church, stood three more projecting chapels, though one of these must have been demolished to make way for the lady chapel, which was added in 1314. The whole church, internally and externally, was finished in the finest limestone, predominantly from Taynton, near Burford in Oxfordshire. It was probably vaulted in stone.

Little of this magnificence remains in the ruins today. However, enough of the south transept and south crossing piers still stands to give some idea of the building's grandeur. Imagine these walls not as rough flint rubble but faced in smooth cut stone, standing to over twice their present height, with finely detailed windows and giant order columns reaching almost to the vaulting. This transept was matched by another on the north of the crossing, while to the west and east stretched the nave and chancel respectively. The floor was covered with beautifully laid, decorated and coloured tiles. Fine carvings, rich furnishings and lavish colour throughout would have completed the impact made on visitors and pilgrims by this great building.

The monastic buildings

A reconstruction of the Abbey showing the square of the cloister just to the south of the nave.

The Abbey church choir was the focus of the monks' prayer and worship (the *Opus Dei*), at eight sacred offices a day. Pilgrims also came to the Abbey church. But it was only one of a number of buildings on the site where the monks ate, slept, worked and studied. The most important of these stood around the cloister, the heart of the community.

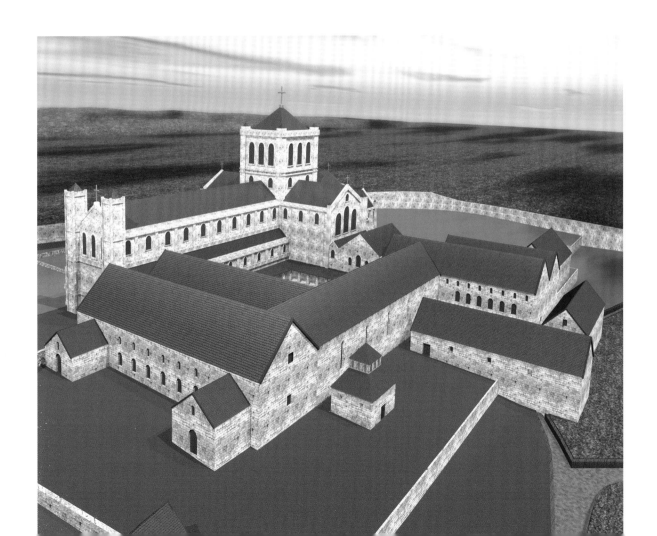

Abbey cloister reconstruction

Opposite page:
A replica capital from the cloister columns painted to show how it might have looked, according to fragments of pigment found on the original stonework.

The cloister gardens today.

The cloister

Virtually nothing remains of the cloister above ground, yet in its day it was one of the glories of the Abbey. Fortunately, enough stones have survived to enable us to recreate it in our imagination in remarkable detail. The cloister was a square with sides of approximately 145 ft (44.2 m). In its centre was an open garden. Around the sides ran a covered walk some 12 ft 6 in (3.8 m) wide, separated from the garden by arcades of single columns supporting intricately carved capitals. Carved springers on these capitals supported round arches made up of more carved stones (voussoirs).

The chapter house

East of the cloister and south of the south transept, from which it was divided by a narrow passage (on the ground floor, possibly with the Abbey treasury on the first), stood the chapter house. This was the official meeting place of the monks, who assembled there every morning to hear a reading from a chapter of the rule of St Benedict (hence the building's name) and religious texts. Parts of the *Opus Dei* would have been sung there. We know from Dr London's visitation of 1538 that the monks still had a daily reading from scripture, often with a homily from the abbot, read to them in the chapter house in both English and Latin.

The chapter house is one of the few structures that remains at its original size. It was 72 ft (22 m) long and 46 ft (14 m) wide and had a vaulted roof perhaps 40 ft (12.3 m) high. In the west wall stood the door, providing access from the cloister walk, flanked by two large windows. Three more windows were set in the wall above. In the apsidal east wall were a further five windows. Around the walls stood benches for the monks (their remains can still be seen), and at the east end were seats for the abbot, prior and sub-prior. It was one of the largest and finest chapter houses in England, and it was here that ecclesiastical councils and other important meetings were held.

Reading's chapter house was probably similar to the one still in use at Bristol Cathedral although the vaulting may have been different.

Passage between the chapter house and the south transept which possibly had the Abbey treasury above it.

Opposite page:
The ruins of the chapter house before, during and after restoration.

Abbey Stones

The 12th-century Abbey church and monastic buildings were built with a core of local flint, faced with cut stone (ashlar), predominantly a hard Jurassic limestone from Taynton, near Burford in Oxfordshire. This honey-coloured stone was used subsequently to build Blenheim, some Oxford Colleges (including Merton and Christ Church) and parts of Windsor Castle. A finer and whiter Jurassic limestone from Caen, Normandy, was used for the capitals and voussoirs in the cloister, whilst Taynton stone was used for most of the springers and column bases. Both facilitated carving and, at Reading Abbey, supported sculpture of a very high quality that demonstrates a high level of skill in masonary and exhibits a remarkable vocabulary of images. This can be seen in the capitals, springers and voussoirs from the cloister now on display in Reading Museum.

The Reading Abbey Stone, used as a font at St James's church, is the only carved stone that was found on site. The cloister stones now in Reading Museum were found during the 20th century in gardens at Holme Park and Borough Marsh, near Sonning, and later at Shiplake. These included the capital carved with the Coronation of the Virgin by Christ, one of the earliest representations in sculpture of this iconic Christian image in western Europe, alongside that in St Swithin's church, Quenington, Gloucestershire. The capital is badly damaged and its full size cannot be ascertained.

Good-quality building stone is rare in Berkshire and South Oxfordshire, where the predominant stone is flint, and in the years following the Dissolution, the Abbey was used as an unofficial quarry. Stone from the Abbey church was used in the mid-16th century for the rebuilding of parts of St Mary's Minster church in Reading, and the Poor Knights' Lodgings at Windsor castle. Elizabeth I's charter to Reading in 1562 gave the corporation the right to remove 200 loads of stone from the Abbey to repair 19 ruinous bridges in the Borough. Further destruction occurred during the Civil War. The last record of stone being taken from the Abbey was for the building of the Conway Bridge at Park Place, Henley, in 1763.

Capital from the Abbey cloister
on display in Reading Museum.

Opposite page:
Carved heads

Capital carved with the Coronation
of the Virgin by Christ.

Stone from the Abbey can be found in walls and buildings around Reading, including the culvert carrying the Holy Brook under the town centre. Carved and cut stones are clearly visible in the grotto in Forbury Gardens, the eastern wall of the gardens linking St James's church to Abbey Walk, and the arch from Forbury Gardens into the Abbey Ruins. These are predominantly Taynton limestone, but not exclusively so: the path linking St James's church to Abbey Walk also features a round cross-section from a Purbeck marble column which would have been in the 13th-century lady chapel.

The 20th-century discovery of the cloister capitals in Sonning and Shiplake is evidence that Abbey stones were put to vernacular use in domestic and garden settings quite widely around Reading. In 2017, the Hidden Abbey Stones project was launched to encourage local people to look out for carved stone which could have come from the Abbey.

The remains of the chapter house and dormitory.

Opposite page:
The view towards the chapter house showing the area that was occupied by the dormitory, with the reredorter – the monks' latrines – in the foreground.

The dormitory

Immediately south of the chapter house was a narrow passage, leading from the cloister probably to the infirmary. The arches that once supported the vaulted roof of the passage can still be seen in the chapter house wall. South of this stood the monks' dormitory. This too was a building on a grand scale. Only the western wall remains, and this only to about half its original height, but enough stands to enable one to recreate it in one's imagination. It was once thought to have been of two storeys, with the sleeping quarters above and a warming room and other monastic offices below, but recent research has suggested that it may have been a single-storey room underneath a vast and high timber roof. The remains of stairs are just visible at the north end of the west wall, which may have led to a room above the passage, or to a dormitory gallery, or possibly to a room above the south aisle of the cloister which, in other monasteries, acted as a scriptorium. The dormitory was built to accommodate up to 200 monks. At the extreme southern end of this block, hard by the river Kennet, can be seen the remains of the reredorter, or monks' latrines.

The Abbey and music

The canon *Sumer is Icumen in* is the oldest known musical round with English words, and the manuscript, held by the British Library, is the earliest known example of a piece of notated music in which both secular and sacred words are written to the same piece of music. The title translates approximately as 'summer (or maybe spring) has arrived'. It is a medieval English round of the mid-13th century, sometimes called the Reading Rota because the earliest known copy of it appears in a manuscript from Reading Abbey which was copied between 1261 and 1264. The same manuscript also gives the name of William de Wycombe, who was the precentor of Reading's daughter priory at Leominster in the 1270s.

Also called the Cuckoo Song or the Summer Canon, it is the first known musical composition featuring six-part polyphony and is possibly the oldest surviving example of independent melodic counterpoint. It is a round composed in the Wessex dialect of Middle English, to be sung by four voices singing the same melody one after the other, accompanied by two lower voices. There are two sets of words: a secular version, in Middle English, written in black, and a sacred version in Latin, written in red. The secular tune and words most probably pre-date the song, which was written down by monks at Reading Abbey in the mid-13th century. There is a 20th-century plaque commemorating *Sumer is Icumen in* in the chapter house.

The manuscript for *Sumer is Icumen in* held in the British Library.

The plaque commemorating the song in the chapter house.

Opposite page:
The restored refectory wall looking much as it must have done originally, as it never had a limestone facing.

The refectory

This stood to the south of the cloister. It was a room of some 167 by 38 ft (51.4 by 11.7 m) and was on the first floor, above a range of cellars. Parliament may have met here. Nothing remains apart from a short stretch of its south wall, visible from the bank below. Like the other monastic buildings (but unlike the church) this always had external walls of finely-cut flint rather than of limestone. The refectory wall gives a good impression of the original appearance.

The inner gateway

The Abbey gateway that we see today is not the original. The arch, which had survived the Dissolution and subsequent depredations better than any other Abbey building, collapsed in spectacular fashion in 1861 in a storm. The present gateway is a restoration, completed later that year under the direction of Sir George Gilbert Scott. However, although it differs in some details from the original, it is sufficiently close in appearance to give us a good idea of what that would have looked like – a large central arch flanked by two pointed windows, with four windows (also probably pointed) lighting a large first-floor hall. This room would have been used by the abbot when, in his capacity as Lord of the Manor of Reading, he held his manorial court.

The original inner gateway (from the south), by an unknown artist.

The collapse of the Abbey gateway in 1861.

The restoration of the gateway was completed in 2018.

Opposite page:
The upper room of the gateway re-opened to the public.

The Hospitium of St John

The central part of the hospitium still stands to the north of St Laurence's graveyard and is currently in use as a day nursery.

The hospitium, a dormitory for visitors, was founded at the end of the 12th century to house the growing number of pilgrims travelling to the Abbey, and also to provide an almshouse for 26 poor men and women (13 of each), together with accommodation for 13 male visitors. The almshouse was next to St Laurence's church. There was also a refectory that was essentially where Reading Town Hall stands now. The hospitium dormitory was set at right angles to the northern end of the refectory; the central part of this is still in existence and currently used as a day nursery.

By the 15th century, there had been a significant decline in the number of pilgrims, and the hospitium was no longer functioning as intended. Edward IV raised the idea of the Abbey establishing a grammar school in the building, and this happened in 1486, at the instigation of Henry VII. The school survived the Dissolution and is now Reading School (today operating from a site on Erleigh Road).

St Laurence's church

St Laurence's church is also still in existence, although much restored both in the 15th and the 19th centuries (and re-worked internally between 2001 and 2004). During the Middle Ages it became a town parish church; it survived the Dissolution and was the Borough church until the 1970s. During the Middle Ages, burials took place north of the Abbey church; Queen Mary Tudor gave St Laurence's its current dedicated churchyard in 1556, 17 years after the Dissolution. Reading Borough Council restored the churchyard wall in 2014.

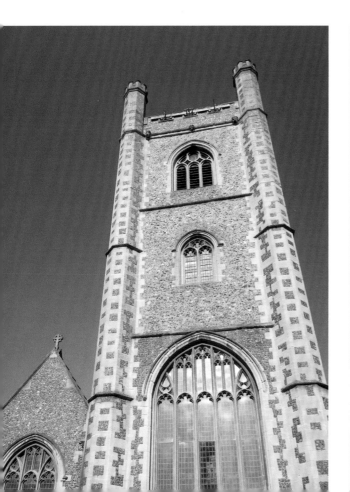

Abbot Hugh Cook Faringdon

Hugh Cook Faringdon was elected on 26 September 1520, having previously been the Abbey's sub-chamberlain. He appears to have been on good terms with King Henry VIII, who visited Reading Abbey two days later to stay for Michaelmas and received from the abbot a generous gift of fish. The king and Abbot Cook continued to exchange gifts until 1539. In 1537 Abbot Cook officiated in the lying-in-state for the dead Queen Jane Seymour.

The process of the Dissolution of the monasteries in England came in two waves: the lesser houses were targeted from 1536 and the greater houses from 1537. The process was led by the king's chief minister, Thomas Cromwell, who, with his son, had been appointed by Abbot Cook as High Steward of Reading Abbey for life in 1536. The Abbey was visited by Cromwell's agents, led by Dr John London, in 1538, who itemised and confiscated the relics. In 1539, Parliament passed an act vesting the possessions of all houses that surrendered in the crown, adding that failure to surrender would be regarded as treason and would result in forfeiture to the crown. Abbot Cook was present in Parliament when this legislation was debated.

Despite this, Cook, along with the abbots of two other great Benedictine houses, Colchester and Glastonbury, did not surrender his abbey. Therefore in October 1539, a writ was issued against Abbot Cook – who had been arrested at his country home, Bere Court (near Pangbourne) – and he was sent to the Tower of London for interrogation. He was sent back to Reading 'to be tried and executed … with his accomplices', two priests, John Eynon (the priest of St Giles's church in Reading) and John Rugge. The trial took place at Reading Abbey, on 13 November 1539, when all three were found guilty of treason for denying the royal supremacy of the English church. They were sentenced to be drawn, hanged and quartered, the punishment for treason, which was carried out on 14 November in the Forbury.

Despite being a Lord Spiritual, Abbot Cook was not tried by his peers, and his sentence was not commuted to mere beheading. The French ambassador, writing on 30 November 1539, told King Francis I that the remains of Abbot Cook were hanged and left in chains outside the Abbey gateway, which suggests that the full sentence of quartering may not have been carried out.

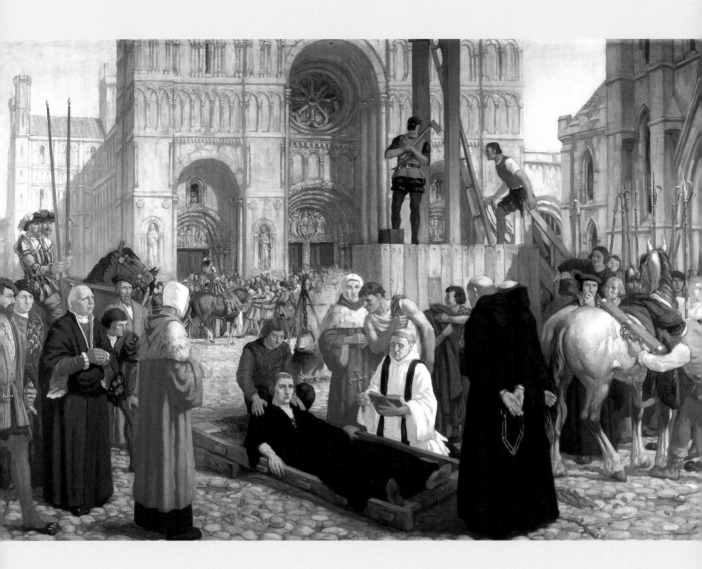

The lost buildings

The west range

Like all monastic cloisters, Reading's was surrounded by buildings on all four sides, but the nature, size and purpose of the west range here remains a mystery. Evidence from other monastic sites suggests that it may have been used by the cellarer.

The abbot's house

The exact location of the abbot's house is not known, but it is believed to have stood close to the inner gateway, on one or the other side of what is now Abbey Street. Nothing survives, and we can only surmise what it was like by comparison with other monastic houses and from the report of the Parliamentary Survey of 1650, which mentions two cellars, two butteries, a hall, a parlour, a dining room, ten chambers, a garret, a large gallery and other small rooms. Clearly, as befitted the abbot of such a prestigious monastery, it was a spacious and comfortable dwelling which accommodated royal and noble guests on a regular basis. After the Dissolution it formed the basis of the Tudor royal palace (see page 65).

The infirmary

This is believed to have stood to the east of the Abbey church, in the grounds of today's prison. Nothing remains, but we can assume from evidence of infirmaries in other abbeys that it contained its own dormitory, refectory, kitchen, chapel, warm room and hall, and was probably adjacent to the Abbey's physic garden which contained herbs and medicinal plants.

The Abbey mill

The ruins of the Abbey mill
adjacent to The Blade office building

The mill stood to the south-west of the monastic buildings, on the southern boundary of the site spanning the Holy Brook. Only two arches remain of the original structure. The mill was substantially rebuilt in 1860 and continued in use until 1959, when everything but the remaining fragments was demolished. In its day, it would have been an important part of the Abbey's working life. Close to the mill stood a bakehouse and a dovecote, both long gone.

The outer gateways

The Abbey precinct covered an area of around 30 acres, bounded to the south by the river Kennet and the Holy Brook. It was surrounded on its east, north and west sides by a stone wall, six feet (1.8m) thick, with four gates giving access. None of these remains, but they were at the following locations:

- the compter gate, the main entrance, at the western end of The Forbury, adjacent to St Laurence's church
- the north or river gate, near the entrance to the Forbury Gardens at the junction of The Forbury and Forbury Road
- the east gate, at the eastern end of Chestnut Walk, close to Blake's Bridge over the River Kennet in Forbury Road
- the south gate, at the junction of Abbey Square and King's Road, opposite the main entrance to Reading Central Library.

The north-eastern part of the Reading Inner Distribution Road (IDR) runs along Forbury Road, which in turn follows the outer line of the Abbey wall from the north gate to the east gate at Blake's Bridge. Parts of the Plummery Wall are retained in the central carriageway wall of the IDR close to the Kenavon Drive roundabout; the plummeries were the Abbey's lead workshops, which were built along the inside of the Abbey wall.

The Plummery Wall

Carved bishop's head, *c.* 1250.
It was found in the Plummery Wall in 1989.

The stables

The stable building stood on the north bank of the Holy Brook between the mill and the south gate, where Reading Central Library is now. As befitted an abbey of Reading's importance, this was a large building some 165 ft (50 m) long and 26 ft (8 m) wide. It was built of flint, with high set windows, and could probably accommodate over 50 horses. Several of these would have been for the use of the abbot and senior servants (the abbot's retinue included a marshall or master of the horse, a huntsman, a palfrey keeper and a carter), but accommodation was also needed for the horses belonging to the Abbey's many important visitors.

Following the Dissolution, the hospitium refectory was converted into stables for the royal palace. The town hall and Blandy & Blandy offices now occupy the site.

The leper house

A leper house was founded in 1134 in a separate building 110 ft (34 m) long and 50 ft (15 m) wide, which would have accommodated a good number of patients. It was dedicated to St Mary Magdalen, as were around 30 other leper houses founded in England and Wales. Its exact location is not known. Foundations discovered during the building of the Assize Courts have been suggested as those of the leper house, but this building could alternatively have been the abbot's house. In recent years an alternative location at Cemetery Junction, on the eastern medieval borough boundary, has been suggested.

THE DECLINE
AND REDISCOVERY
OF THE ABBEY QUARTER

Linenfold panelling originally from Reading Abbey now resides in Magdalen College Dining Hall, Oxford.

Opposite page:
St Mary's church which also fell into disrepair after Dissolution and was extensively restored in 1551–55 using stone and timber from the ruined Abbey. The north door is probably from the cloister and there are records in the churchwarden's accounts of the purchase of a roof and pillars from the 'Abbye' which are probably the current nave roof and the pillars that separate the nave from the south aisle.

The Dissolution

Reading Abbey was dissolved in September 1539, in the second wave (see page 52) of the Dissolution, which targeted the greater houses. The Reading town records indicate that the Abbey had been suppressed and the abbot, Hugh Cook Faringdon, deprived of his abbacy on 18 September 1539. He was executed two months later.

After Dissolution the Abbey passed into royal ownership, and William Penizon and Thomas Vachell (a Berkshire man) were appointed as custodians. Vachell, as deputy High Steward of the Abbey, took over the role the abbot had held as Lord of the Manor, and in October 1539 he administered the oath to the incoming mayor in the monastery great hall, probably in the abbot's house. The king granted Reading a charter in 1542 that gave the burgesses the right to elect their own mayor. The right to hold annual fairs (which had fallen to two, many years before) was granted to Penizon, who became Chief Steward of the Borough after Cromwell's fall in 1540; these were to continue to be held in the Forbury.

The Abbey church appears to have been taken out of use and locked. It was kept structurally intact, subject to the removal of demountable fittings, such as the 16th-century linenfold panelling now in the Hall of Magdalen College Oxford which, according to both the college and Pevsner, came from Reading Abbey, and which the college bought from a secondary source in 1540.

Henry VIII continued to use the abbot's house and related monastic buildings as royal accommodation, and it was maintained as such. New royal stables were established in the dormitory of the hospitium.

The Abbey's ownership changed following Henry VIII's death in 1547. Under his young son, Edward VI (1547–53), the lordship of Reading and the ownership of the Abbey was granted to the new king's uncle, the Duke of Somerset, in July 1548. He started the process of degrading the Abbey church and cloister, stripping the roofs of lead and offering this and the bells for sale, melted down, along with other Abbey facilities including the windows, stone and tiles, and the monks' toilets ('Jakes stoles'). Stone and tiles from the Abbey choir were used to rebuild the south aisle of St Mary's church, Reading (Reading Minster). It is likely that it was at this time, when the choir was being dismantled, that

the tomb of Henry I and other royal tombs were broken up. Dr Jamieson Hurry, in *Reading Abbey*, refers to the workmen unsuccessfully searching for the silver coffin in which the king was rumoured to have been buried, rifling his tomb and scattering his remains.

Accounts of these transactions were kept, and in 1552 were cited as evidence in the trial of Somerset for felony, for which he was subsequently executed. It is sometimes suggested that Somerset is the Duke after whom Duke Street was named.

Education and the Abbey

Reading School

It is maintained that Reading School was founded, as part of Reading Abbey, in 1125. It had ceased to function by the 15th century, when there was pressure on the Abbey to re-found a school. The 'Free Grammar School' was established by Abbot John Thorne, at the encouragement of King Henry VII, in 1486, in the hospitium dormitory. In this context, 'free' means the teaching of the liberal arts, not an absence of fees.

The school survived the Dissolution of the Abbey. At the time its master was Dr Leonard Cox, a leading humanist and a scholar of international reputation in Europe, who was the author of the first book in English on rhetoric. He was appointed by Abbot Cook in 1530 and continued at Reading School until 1546.

At the Dissolution, the school was transferred to the corporation of Reading. Elizabeth I, in her charter to Reading of 1560, made the corporation responsible for the master's appointment and payment.

Reading School, 1816.
A colour postcard by Thomas Thorp, based on the print entitled 'View of Reading School & Playground' by Edmund Havell.

The school continued to operate from the hospitium until 1786, sharing the premises with the corporation from 1578. The boys made regular use of the Forbury's open space for sport, including cricket.

In 1786 the school was moved into new premises elsewhere in the Forbury area by its energetic headteacher, Dr Richard Valpy, sometimes known as 'the Mighty Flogger', while the hospitium continued to be used to house boarders until 1866. The school prospered in its new site in the early years of the 19th century but then went into decline under Valpy's son, closing briefly in 1866 when, according to legend, the inspectors, on asking to see the school, were told, 'He's runned (sic) away'. It was re-founded by the Reading School Act 1867 and moved to Erleigh Road in 1871, into new buildings designed for it by Alfred Waterhouse.

Reading University College

In 1878 the hospitium was bought for the Borough by the mayor, Arthur Hill, and put to use as a junior library. It was subsequently renovated to accommodate the Reading Schools of Science and Art, which later became the University Extension College (see page 74). St Laurence's vicarage, located to the east of the hospitium in Valpy Street, was bought by the University Extension College in the 1890s and linked to the hospitium by a new building in 1893/94. The British Dairy Institute moved to the site in 1896, and new buildings linking the Institute to the College were opened at the corner of Valpy Street and The Forbury in 1898, by the Prince of Wales. In 1902 the complex was awarded University College status; the site was therefore the first home of what is now the University of Reading. It was short-lived, however, as the University College started the move to its London Road campus in 1906, after which the British Dairy Institute building was taken over by Reading Council as its police station. It was demolished in 1981, when the site was developed for offices.

Abbey School

During the 18th century, the Reading Ladies' Boarding School operated in the Abbey gateway and adjacent buildings. The school was attended by Jane Austen and her sister Cassandra between 1785 and 1786; at that time the Abbey School was ruled by a Mrs La Tournelle, who had a cork leg and a passion for theatre. By 1850 the school had moved out, and the gateway was in divided ownership. The Council bought both parts by 1860 to secure the building, which was in a dangerous state of repair. The archway collapsed in 1861 and the council commissioned Sir George Gilbert Scott to restore the building, which he comprehensively achieved by 1862.

National School

A National School was built in 1812 against the northern wall inside the ruins of the chapter house, following a local subscription. Such development was possible because the Abbey Ruins were, at that time, in private hands. The school was demolished in 1837. A new National School (St Laurence's School) was built in Abbey Street in 1852. This was closed in 1927 and subsequently demolished.

The Abbey gateway, restored in 2018.

St Laurence's School in Abbey Street c. 1960, prior to being demolished.

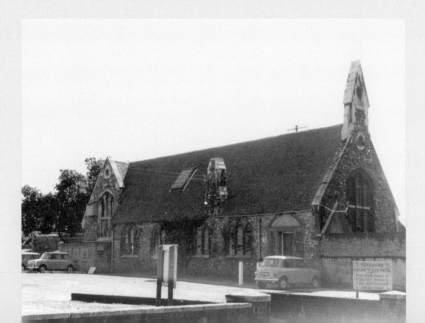

Portrait of Queen Elizabeth I
by an unkonwn artist, around 1575.

The royal palace

Edward VI stayed in the Abbey, by now called the *Kynges place*, in 1552. Under Edward VI's successor, Mary Tudor (1553–58), the Abbey reverted to the crown, and Sir Francis Englefield, a local Berkshire man and staunch Catholic, was appointed as keeper. Mary stayed at the Abbey in 1554 with her new husband, Philip of Spain, whom she had married that year in Winchester. She did not restore the Abbey as a monastic community, and during her reign stone from the lady chapel was taken to Windsor to assist the building of the Poor Knights' Lodgings in the castle in 1557. Mary granted land in the Forbury to St Laurence's church for a dedicated graveyard in 1556.

Elizabeth I (1558–1603) granted a new charter to Reading in 1560 that formed the basis of the town's civic rights until the 19th century. Englefield, as a Catholic, fled the country, and the queen granted many of his duties to the corporation. The charter gave the corporation rights over St Laurence's church and the hospitium, including the grammar school, and reaffirmed the right to hold four fairs a year in the Forbury (the third fair had been revived and a fourth granted under Edward VI and Somerset) which, by implication, gave the corporation rights of use over parts of the Forbury. The corporation also took possession of the compter gate – the main entrance to the Abbey precinct on the south side of St Laurence's church – including the former Abbey prison linked to the gate.

Under Henry VIII the corporation had moved their guild hall from Yield Hall Lane into the church of the dissolved Greyfriars friary in Friar Street. This too they found unsatisfactory, and by 1578 the corporation had moved to the hospitium dormitory, which it now shared with the grammar school. An upper storey was added to the great hall, with the corporation upstairs and the school on the ground floor. This state of affairs continued for the next 200 years, with the occasional dispute about noise and the use by the school of the Forbury for sport and recreation.

Elizabeth continued the destruction of the Abbey church, with stone being used for the repair of roads and bridges in the Borough, including Caversham

Opposite page:

The Forbury today

Bridge (under the provisions of the 1560 charter). She repaired and extended the abbot's house, now called the Queen's House. She stayed in Reading on at least ten occasions between 1568 and 1603, including in her final months.

After Elizabeth's death, her successor, James I (1603–25), granted the Abbey to his wife, Anne of Denmark, but neither stayed in the palace. Their son, Charles I (1625–49), was the last king to reside there, doing so with the court for Michaelmas term in 1625. A second visit, planned for 1629, did not happen.

Civil War

The English Civil War (1642–46) brought hardship and destruction to the town of Reading. Located in the Thames Valley between Parliament in London and the king in Oxford, Reading had a strategic military importance to both sides. Initially held by Parliament, Reading was occupied for the king in November 1642 and then defended by a Royalist garrison under Sir Arthur Aston. The parliamentary army, under the Earl of Essex, laid siege to Reading in April 1643, and the town surrendered to the Parliamentarians. Essex then occupied Reading but withdrew to London in September 1643, when the Royalists returned. The king decided to abandon Reading in May 1644, at which time the Royalists slighted the town's defences.

During this period, both sides – but principally Aston – raised defensive works around the town that cut through the Abbey. Aston built a rampart and a ditch that ran through the cloister and nave from south to north to end in a defensive position (redan) around the Forbury hill. Stone from the Abbey was used to construct the rampart and mound, and parts of the north transept (now in the St James's church precinct) may have been brought down by mining and explosion, either to provide more stone or to remove an obstruction to the view commanding the Thames to the east. Other damage may have been caused during the ten days of bombardment that preceded the Royalist surrender. The Civil War was a significant cause of the Abbey ruins taking on their present-day appearance.

With the Commonwealth (1649–60), Reading Abbey came under parliamentary jurisdiction. A survey of 1650 records the existence and use of the old Abbey stable block (where Reading Central Library now is); the Abbey mill; the porter's lodge by the compter gate (to the south of St Laurence's church); the former royal residence in the abbot's house, including the inner Abbey gateway; and associated outbuildings. The Forbury was also recorded as a walled area where the town held four fairs. In 1652, the corporation took responsibility for levelling the defensive ditch in the Forbury to enable the 1653 cattle fair to be held there on St James's Day.

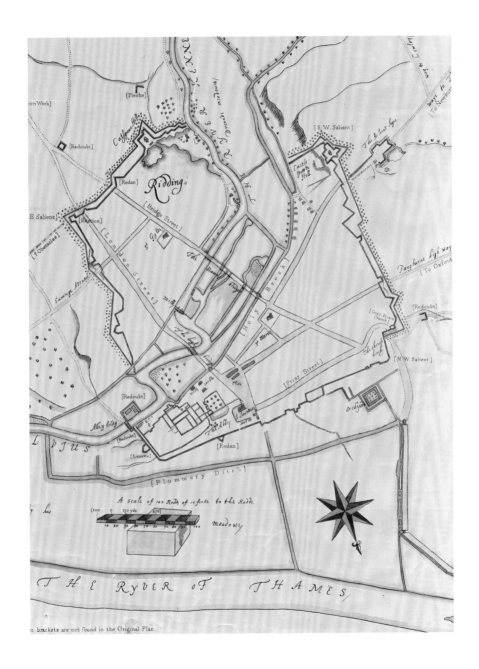

[orn Work]

[Fleche]

[Redoubt]

Coffenst Hills

[Redan]

Ridding

E. Salient

[Bastion]

[Bridge Street]

[? Obstacles]

[London Street]

Savinge Avenue

[Redoubt]

Abey bridg

[Redoubt]

[Lunette]

[Redan]

L V I U S

[Plummery Ditch]

The Holy Brook

S.W. Salient

Castle Streets Mill

Pangburst high way

[To Oxford]

[Grey Friars Church]

[Redoubt]

N W Salient

Friar Street

Orchyard

[S.W. Salient]

way to Newbury

[To Newbu...]

A scale of 100 Rodds of 16 foote to the Rodde.
100   0   150 yds   450

meadowy

T H E   R Y V E R   o F   T H A M E S

n brackets are not found in the Original Plan.

69

Post-restoration

A naive view of the ruins of Reading Abbey. Watercolour by Mary Webster, 16 August 1849.

Ownership of the Abbey returned to the crown in 1660, but royal interest in a palace in Reading was not renewed. From 1661 the Abbey land was sold or leased into private hands, while the corporation defended its right to hold four fairs a year in the Forbury and the school used the Forbury for recreation. From the late 17th century, private houses, including Pageant House (now demolished) were built around the Forbury.

By the 18th century, the Abbey had become a picturesque ruin, drawn by antiquarians, though it was still seen by some to have value as a quarry. By the mid-18th century the ownership of the land had been consolidated in the hands of two families: the Vansittarts to the east of the inner Abbey gateway and the Blagraves to the west.

Forbury renaissance

In his book *The History and Antiquities of Reading* (1802) Coates includes an updated and embellished version of Englefield's plan.

In 1779, Sir Henry Englefield published his survey of the Abbey precinct, based on his archeological investigation, which has been the basis of our knowledge of the layout of the site ever since.

The interest his work stimulated led to a focus on the Abbey quarter as an integral part of the town centre which has continued into the 21st century and given to the town some excellent examples of 19th-century architecture in the Forbury area, of which Reading can be justifiably proud.

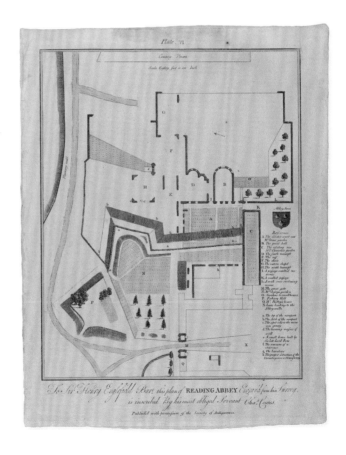

Reading Gaol

In the 1780s it was decided to replace the inadequate county and borough prisons in Reading (in Castle Street, where the other St Mary's church – Church of England Continuing – is now; and Greyfriars in Friar Street, respectively) by a new County House of Correction, which was built and opened in 1786 on land to the east of the Abbey ruins, on the site of the lady chapel and monks' cemetery. In due course this proved inadequate, and the site was redeveloped as the Reading gaol between 1842 and 1844. The new gaol was built to a design based on the New Model Prison of Pentonville and followed the 'separate system' of punishment, where prisoners were kept in solitary confinement. The design was by Sir George Gilbert Scott and W.B. Moffat, it being one of Scott's early works.

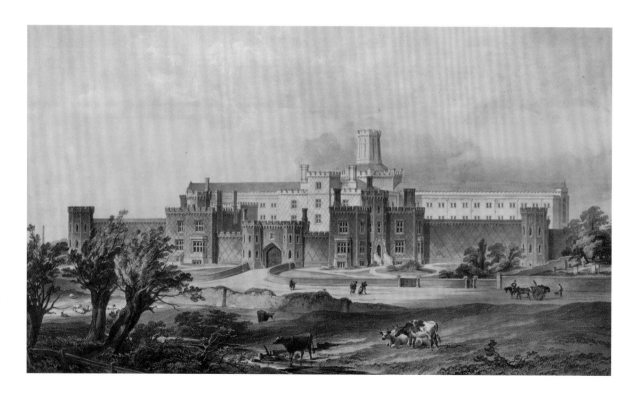

Reading Town Hall

Also in the 1780s, the corporation and the grammar school had outgrown their shared use of the hospitium, and both made plans to move. In 1785 the corporation moved into a new town hall and council chamber, designed by Charles Poulton, an Alderman, and built on the site of the hospitium refectory. This is the core of the current Reading Town Hall complex, including what is now called Victoria Hall. A year later the school also moved (see pages 63 and 74).

The town hall was extended between 1874 and 1876 by the provision of the new municipal buildings and clock tower in Blagrave Street. These were designed by Alfred Waterhouse, the architect of the Natural History Museum in London, who lived and practised in Reading and West Berkshire.

Reading School and University

The Schools of Science and Art and the administrative headquarters of the University Extension College in the old hospitium, with St Laurence's vicarage beyond.

The construction of the new town hall in the 1780s cut out light from the grammar school on the ground floor of the hospitium. The Headmaster, Richard Valpy, therefore built – at his own expense – a new school house in what is now Blagrave Street. It was in use from 1786, while the school continued to use the hospitium for boarders.

The school moved again, in 1871, to its current site on Erleigh Road. This left the old hospitium bereft of use. In 1878 it was bought for the borough and subsequently occupied by the newly-founded Schools of Science and Art which became the University Extension College in 1892; thus the hospitium was the original home of the institution which was to become the University of Reading.

St James's church

Reading had a purpose-built Roman Catholic chapel from 1811; unfortunately, it was on a proposed route of the Great Western Railway. Between 1837 and 1840 James Wheble, a local Catholic antiquarian and landowner, therefore commissioned Augustus Pugin to build a replacement church on land owned by Wheble, north of the north transept of the Abbey. The church was dedicated to St James and built in Romanesque style, the only such example of Pugin's work in Great Britain, and his first major ecclesiastical design. Both side aisles have been added in the 20th century.

Pugin also designed the presbytery and possibly a school, built in flint from the Abbey, to the south of the church, with the presbytery on the line of the north transept. A replacement school was built in 1872–74 on the site of the Abbey church chancel and choir. It is now a day nursery.

Pugin's St James's church complex completes the group of buildings by three great Victorian architects (Pugin, Waterhouse and Scott) that graces the Forbury area.

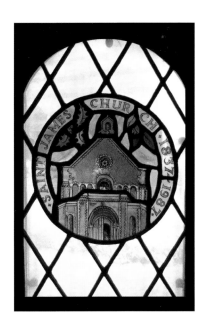

19th-century consolidation

Town houses on Abbots Walk

James Wheble was significant in securing the Forbury and the Abbey ruins from urban development and as a civic and historic amenity for the town.

At the turn of the 19th century, the eastern part of the Abbey quarter, including part of the Abbey gateway, the cloister and refectory, and the chapter house to the south, was primarily in the hands of the Vansittart family. In the 1830s Nicholas Vansittart, Lord Bexley, was developing plans to clear the area and demolish part of the ruins to construct new access roads and houses. This stimulated local opposition and a public subscription to buy this part of the site for the town, which raised enough to buy the south transept and the chapter house. Wheble bought the cloister, the eastern section of the inner gateway and the eastern part of the Forbury from Bexley in 1835, after it had become clear that the corporation was unlikely to raise more funds. Although Bexley's plans were not realised, a number of elegant town houses were built along the southern boundary of the Forbury, three of which remain in Abbots Walk. Wheble undertook archaeological excavations of the Abbey chancel and choir, where he discovered the Reading Abbey Stone that he later gave to St James's church to serve as a font, where it can still be seen.

James Wheble died in 1840, and in 1854, his son James Joseph sold his remaining land in the Abbey quarter to the corporation. This included the cloister, the eastern part of the Forbury and Forbury Hill. At this stage, the western part of the Forbury (including the western part of the Abbey gateway) remained in the hands of the Blagrave family and was still being used by the council to hold fairs. The council completed this purchase in 1860.

In 1859, the council also bought the remainder of the Abbey Ruins – the dormitory, reredorter and what is now Chestnut Walk – from a third private owner, the Bunscombe family. Thus by 1860 the council had secured public ownership of what we now know as Forbury Gardens and the Abbey Ruins, and established a route from the gardens through the ruins to Chestnut Walk and the north bank of the River Kennet. To facilitate this, James Joseph Wheble and St James's church donated a strip of land to the corporation to allow a tunnel to be built from the gardens into the Abbey Ruins. This incorporated Abbey stonework in the arches.

The eastern part of Forbury Gardens was opened officially as a pleasure garden in 1861. Forbury Hill became the location of a Crimean War cannon. The eastern and western parts of the Forbury were still separated physically by a wall which was not removed until 1869/70, after which the gardens were managed as one public garden. In 1871, the corporation undertook repairs to the walls of the Abbey Ruins, using cement (see page 89).

The Maiwand Lion was erected in 1886. Designed by George Blackall Simonds, a member of the local brewing family, it commemorated the involvement of what later became the Royal Berkshire Regiment in the Battle of Maiwand in 1880 during the Second Afghan war, where the regiment suffered heavy losses. The bandstand was provided in 1896, and the Victoria Gates were installed in 1897 to commemorate the Queen's Diamond Jubilee.

The later 19th and early 20th centuries saw the development of more public buildings in the Abbey quarter surrounding Forbury Gardens, in particular along The Forbury. New Assize Courts – now the Reading Crown Court – were built and opened to the west of the Abbey gateway in 1861, with a new county police station at the rear, designed by the County Surveyor John Berry Clacy. Berkshire County Council was established as a local government administrative body in 1889 and built a new Shire Hall next to the Assize Court in 1909–11, in a municipal William-and-Mary style; this is now the Forbury

Hotel. Both buildings were sited so as not to obstruct the view of the gateway along Abbots Walk.

Sutton's Seeds had their offices, packing and distribution centre on the south side of The Forbury, to the west of the Shire Hall. Beyond this stood the late 17th-century Pageant House (also known as Forbury House). This area has been re-developed several times since and is now occupied by Forbury Square and Davidson House, opened in 2003.

These developments benefited from the opening up of the Forbury into the – formerly walled – Abbey precinct area from the north end of Market Place. A new road ran through the area of the old compter or west gate of the Abbey, along the south side of St Laurence's church, This involved the demolition of the south transept chapel of the church which would have intruded across the line of the road, and also of the Blagrave Piazza, a public shelter that ran along the south wall of the nave at the top of Market Place. This re-modelling occurred in 1867–68.

A holy space

There are few records of the Abbey Ruins being used for specifically religious purposes before the 20th century. Towards the end of the 19th century, increased interest in the Abbey and its religious history did see visits from literary and archaeological groups such as that of the Oxford Archaeological and Architectural Society in 1879. The development of the University Extension College in Reading attracted a new inquisitive group interested in discovering more about all aspects of the Abbey's history, and Dr Hurry's work raised the profile of the Abbey as a religious institution as well as interest in its architectural importance.

In the 20th century the Abbey site hosted several religious events. In 1905 the Anglican Diocesan Missionary Festival held a meeting and service in the ruins. In 1909 the Catholics organised a procession around the Abbey precinct on Palm Sunday. This caused a great deal of upset in the town as it was illegal at that time for Catholics to hold processions with their clergy in vestments and carrying the host, the consecrated wafer that Catholics believe is the body of Christ. It outraged many Protestants in the town, and legal action was threatened. The next year the Catholics organised a 'pilgrimage' to the ruins but there appears to have been less dissension. A service was held in the ruins, after which a procession went to the station, led by a thurifer and with acolytes carrying candles, behind whom the people followed, two deep, singing Marian hymns and reciting the rosary.

In 1914 the Primitive Methodists held a service in the ruins, and in 1916 the Salvation Army marked its 51st anniversary there.

Although political gatherings were not permitted, religious events were allowed. For instance, the Catholics held regular processions and services in the ruins during the inter-war period, The Reading and District Free Church Council held an annual Easter service there, and the Salvation Army once again met in the ruins in 1935, with General Evangeline Booth in attendance.

The centenary of the founding of St James's church fell in 1941, while Britain was at war. Despite this, and no doubt under the threat of an air raid, a large gathering was held on the nearest Sunday to the feast of St James (25 July).

Opposite page:
A Mass to celebrate the centenary
of St James's church was held in
the ruins in 1941.

The Palm Sunday Procession in 1909;
the photograph shows the gathering
outside St James's church. Note the
donkey in the foreground.

Abbot Mooney seated surrounded
by the clergy and people at the 1941
Mass to celebrate the centenary
of St James's church.

This was on Sunday 27 July, and Abbot Mooney from the local Benedictine
Abbey of Douai presided over a Pontifical High Mass in the ruins. One notable
person in attendance was Father John Heenan; known as the 'radio priest', he
later became Cardinal Archbishop of Westminster.

After the war the Catholics of Reading frequently used the ruins for various
services. The most regular was the annual Corpus Christi procession. One of
Reading's most populous incomer communities is the Polish. During and after
the war, this included those fleeing first Nazi-invaded Poland and then the
Communist regime. In more recent times, following the collapse of communism
and Poland's membership of the European Union, there has been an influx of
a younger generation. In both cases they joined the existing local Catholic
population – many descended from Irish and Italian families – in keeping the
traditions alive. The participants gathered outside the Polish church of the
Sacred Heart in Watlington Street in 2006 and processed the short distance to
the ruins where benediction, the blessing of the congregation with the host,
was accompanied by singing. The Catholic congregation was joined by those of
other faiths who came together to celebrate a shared spiritual heritage.

The Abbey was built as a sacred space, a place for reflection. It lay dormant
for several hundred years, but since the late 19th century, many groups have
found it once again to be a place for contemplation. Traditions dating back
over a thousand years have been brought back to Reading; one such is the use
of the scallop shell, the emblem of pilgrimage. It figured on the coat of arms
of Reading Abbey and today is used by St James's church and the University
of Reading. The grooves on the scallop shell of St James, the pilgrim's badge,
may be interpreted as representing the many ways in which people of all faiths
and none can join together in celebrating a shared heritage in the Abbey ruins.

20th century

The three memorial tablets in
the chapter house of the restored
Abbey Ruins.

Abbots' memorial in the chapter
house.

Opposite page:
Abbey Wharf

Reading Town Hall

Interest in the history of the Abbey grew during this period, encouraged primarily by Dr Jamieson Hurry, a local medical man, who published his definitive book, *Reading Abbey,* in 1900. In 1909 Dr Hurry donated the memorial cross to Henry I which is still located in Forbury Gardens, on the site of the nave of the destroyed Abbey church. In 1911, Hurry also gave two memorial tablets, located on the inner walls of the chapter house, to commemorate the first and last abbots; a third memorial tablet was added in 1913 to commemorate *Sumer is Icumen in.*

Reading Museum's collection of ten paintings depicting key events in the history of Reading Abbey were commissioned by Dr Hurry from 1890 onwards and can still be seen in the Town Hall and Museum galleries.

Following World War I, a new war memorial was erected at the Victoria Gates in 1931. During World War II, an air-raid shelter for St James's school was constructed in the dormitory area of the Abbey ruins.

Abbey Place and wharf

In the 1970s, Berkshire County Council made proposals for new high-rise offices on land that it owned to the south of the Crown Court, alongside the Abbey wharf on the River Kennet. The proposals were strongly opposed locally and were not approved. In 1980/81 the county council moved out of the centre of Reading to a purpose-built new Shire Hall at Shinfield Park (now the Foster Wheeler headquarters). The area south of the Abbey gateway was redeveloped to a less intrusive scale in the 1980s, including the construction of Abbots House (now a flagship office for Deloitte UK and Boyes Turner) in a neo-Georgian pastiche style in Abbots Walk, possibly on the site of the former abbot's house and the western part of the cloister. This development included a new garden – privately owned but with public access – on the south-eastern side of the cloister, with views over the Abbey Ruins to the east; and new offices on the Abbey wharf on the west bank of the River Kennet, north of Queen's Road.

Reading Town Hall

In 1977, Reading Borough Council started to move its operation from the town hall as part of a major urban redevelopment scheme of the area between Castle Street and Oxford Road to the west of St Mary's Butts and the original Saxon settlement, which also included The Butts shopping centre (now Broad Street Mall). By the end of the century, the town hall was in need of major investment. This came about through a successful bid for a Millennium Lottery grant of £4.11m, which allowed the town hall, concert hall, museum and art gallery to be refurbished and re-opened to the public in 2000 at a total cost of £5.1m.

Reading Gaol

Reading Gaol experienced a number of changes of use during the 20th century, including a period in the 1920s and 30s during which it was mothballed, followed by use as a wartime detention centre by the Canadian armed forces and then as a borstal, a local prison, and latterly as a Young Offender Institution. It was closed in 2013.

The 19th-century exterior wall with its gatehouse and turrets, designed by Sir George Gilbert Scott, was demolished and replaced in the early 1970s by a more utilitarian perimeter wall. As part of this process, Cecil Slade from the University of Reading carried out an archaeological excavation of the north side of the choir ambulatory of the Abbey church within the prison walls, in 1971–73, which uncovered the footings of the northern side of the ambulatory, including one apsidal side chapel which had not featured on the Englefield plans of 1779.

A view of the Blade through a gap in the dormitory wall.

Abbey mill and stables

In the 1980s, Berkshire County Council revised the eastern route of the proposed Reading Inner Distribution Road (IDR), originally intended to run through the western edge of the Forbury Gardens, to pass along the northern and eastern boundaries of the precinct. This new dual-carriageway route, opened in 1989, has preserved and reinforced the integrity of the Abbey Quarter and includes in its central reservation the remains of the Plummery Wall, which followed the Plummery Brook, the Abbey's northern boundary. The IDR now crosses the Kennet at the site of the Abbey's east gate, where there was a bridge that was sometimes called Blakes Bridge.

The change of route for the IDR opened up the old Abbey stables site for development. In 1983–86 Berkshire County Council, which a decade earlier had taken over responsibility for the borough's library service, built the new Reading Central Library on this site. This building straddles the Holy Brook, which can still be seen on either side of it.

The Abbey mill, which had remained operational since the Dissolution, was closed and demolished (apart from the mill arch) in 1959. The site is now occupied by The Blade, a high-rise office block and new Reading landmark.

Forbury Gardens and Abbey Ruins

The Forbury Gardens, looking north.

The ruins were listed as a Scheduled Ancient Monument in 1915, and the Abbey precinct was so listed in 1957 under Town and Country Planning legislation. Reading Abbey, as a Cluniac and Benedictine monastery and Civil War earthwork, is now scheduled under the Ancient Monuments and Archaeological Areas Act 1979 as a site of national importance.

Reading Borough Council started a comprehensive repair programme in 1967 that was subsequently discontinued, and by 1982 the ruins were found to be unsafe and closed to regular public access. This stimulated the foundation of the Friends of Reading Abbey. Prompted by the Friends, and in conjunction with the Public Buildings and Works section of the Department of the Environment, the council ran a comprehensive repair project between 1985 and 1991 which consolidated the ruins and brought them back into public use, but did so through the use of cement rather than lime mortar, with unfortunate consequences (see page 89).

The Abbey Ruins have latterly acquired a number of specific uses, including the annual Corpus Christi procession for the Roman Catholic churches in Reading, and the Progress Theatre's annual performances of 'Shakespeare in the Ruins' in the chapter house.

Following the millennium restoration and re-opening of Reading Town Hall, the council turned its attention to Forbury Gardens and succeeded in attracting Heritage Lottery funding for their restoration between 2003–05. This did not include the Abbey Ruins, but did involve the installation of a new arch over the doorway from the south aisle of the nave to the cloister.

A further survey of the Abbey Ruins in 2008 by Oxley Conservation (Henley), funded by English Heritage, identified a problem with flints spalling from the conserved Abbey walls, which could put passers-by at risk. This resulted in the ruins being closed again to the public in 2009 and permanently fenced off. The problem was directly attributable to the use of cement capping in earlier restoration projects which did not absorb rain water but caused it to run down the walls, leeching the older mortar below and making flints unstable.

At the same time, the Council identified problems with the Abbey gateway.

In the 1860s restoration by Sir George Gilbert Scott, guttering and drainpipes had been built into the structure to hide their unsightly presence. As a consequence, their subsequent failure and leakage had not been noticed, and the building had suffered from serious water ingress.

Following careful assessment of the work required, the council made a successful bid to the Heritage Lottery Fund. Together with funding from the council itself, this provided £3.1m for the project known as *Reading Abbey Revealed.* This encompassed the conservation and re-opening to the public of the Abbey Ruins and surrounding parkland, and the repair and re-opening of the Abbey gateway, all supported by an improved programme of interpretation and signage to bring the Abbey to life and to signpost it from key parts of the town centre, including Reading station and The Oracle shopping centre.

To support and inform the Heritage Lottery bidding process, in 2011 Reading Borough Council developed an action plan for the whole of the newly conceived 'Abbey Quarter', including Town Hall Square and the Market Place, which is the blueprint for its conservation and forward development. Within this blueprint, and alongside *Reading Abbey Revealed,* the council has promoted or funded a number of key projects to enhance the Abbey Quarter, including:

- the restoration of the Simeon Monument (lamp post) in Market Place, designed in 1804 by another great British architect, Sir John Soane (2007)

- the re-paving of Town Hall Square, and the conservation of the St Laurence's drinking fountain and the Queen Victoria statue (2013)

- the restoration and reconstruction of the St Laurence's churchyard wall along The Forbury (2015)

- the relocation of the Spanish Civil War memorial from outside the old Civic Offices to the east end of Forbury Gardens (2015)

- the installation of the new Trooper Potts VC memorial on The Forbury, opposite the Crown Court (2015).

The conservation of the Abbey Ruins

Painstaking repair work
was undertaken in 2017/18.

In the 1980s Reading Borough Council raised money to carry out comprehensive repairs to the Abbey Ruins which were deteriorating. The thinking at that time was that the best way to protect the walls was to add an impervious cap on top to act like a coping, to shed water and stop the original wall getting saturated. This was done using flint and a strong mortar made with a mixture of Portland cement and lime. Unfortunately, over time, this strong but brittle 'hard cap' developed cracks as it expanded and contracted in different weather conditions and water then got trapped in the wall. In addition to this, water running down the hard capping eroded the original softer wall face below and encouraged plants such as buddleia to establish. The woody roots of this plant are particularly damaging. Annual inspections to kerb this growth and the damage associated with it struggled to keep up with the progressive deterioration.

In 2009, with help from a grant from Historic England, a series of experimental repairs were done on a section of the dormitory wall to see what alternatives there might be for longer-lasting conservation of the ruins. These included re-pointing in natural hydraulic lime mortar, using lime-based, thrown 'harling' to consolidate large areas of unstable wall face and placing turf and sedum 'soft cappings' on top of the wall. Soft cappings are a natural and effective way of protecting the tops of the walls from frost damage and mitigating rain water run-off by absorbing water like a sponge and then gradually releasing it. The trial repairs were annually monitored and have generally been left alone during the subsequent conservation work so that this can continue. The thrown harling, if used comprehensively, would make a dramatic change to the appearance of the ruins and it is now understood that it has not necessarily tackled the underlying instability of the wall face.

Following these repair trials it was realised that an increasing number of flints were dropping off the walls and so the ruins had to be closed to the public until consolidation work could be done to make them safe again. A comprehensive condition survey was carried out in 2011 using scaled 'photogrammetric' elevation images derived from a laser scan to identify the varying condition of the wall faces and measure the different areas. These were then translated into a schedule of repairs which could be priced. The elevations were also used by the project's 'above ground' archaeologist Stuart Harrison, archaeologist to York Minster and an authority on Romanesque architecture, to identify evidence of former architectural features in the visible indentations left in the walls by the robbed facing stones. Their outlines were then superimposed on the elevations of the ruins. This process uncovered hitherto unknown details of the lost Abbey church and monastic buildings and, later on, helped the conservation masons preserve as much as possible of this physical evidence.

The design and conservation work on the Abbey Ruins was part of a larger project, 'Reading Abbey Revealed', enabled by a Heritage Lottery Fund grant, which included the ruins, repairs and alterations to the Abbey gateway, interpretation and wayfinding across the Abbey Quarter, a new permanent exhibition at Reading Museum and an extensive programme of related activities.

Repairing the chapter house
in 2017/18.

Following general conservation practice the repair trials used lime mortar made with natural hydraulic lime (NHL) on the assumption that this was compatible with the lime mortar used in the original building. Hydraulic lime contains clays and other 'impurities' that allow it to set in wet conditions, whereas mortars made with pure quick lime rely on absorbing carbon dioxide from the air to cure gradually. In fact, lime used for building in the past always contained some impurities because it was derived from locally quarried limestone, which gave the mortar some hydraulic properties. Recent research has established that the production methods used for the manufacture of modern NHL creates such a strong set over time that mortars made with it end up as hard and impermeable as cement mortar. Historic England are now promoting the use of what is known as 'hot mix' lime mortar made with quick lime, sand and water. The processes of slaking the quick lime and mixing the mortar are combined into one operation, as was done historically, to produce mortar with physical properties more compatible with the original fabric. Further tests with hot mixes on the ruins led to the introduction of a small

The turf 'soft capping' protecting the top of the chapter house walls.

proportion of brick dust into the mix, to mimic the strength-giving impurities found in locally burnt lime. Larger stones were also introduced into the mix to help fill the irregular joints between flints in the rubble walls.

The conservation work on the ruins was done in phases, starting with the transept and chapel walls at the north end of the site, moving on to the chapter house and refectory wall and finishing with the dormitory at the south end. The lower parts of the walls, where indentations from the original facing stones are still visible, were carefully patched with mortar. The soot-blackened crust caused by centuries of coal burning made it easy to distinguish between surfaces dating back to the dismantling of the Abbey in the sixteenth century and more recently damaged areas. Rare examples of surviving facing stones, and the 'tails' left in the wall when facing stones broke as they were removed, were shelter-coated with a fine slurry of lime mortar and sand to protect the stone face from further erosion.

Halfway up the walls there was a clearly visible stripe of erosion caused by the water run-off from above. This is where the most plants, including buddleia, were found growing in the walls. Much of the face layer had to be removed so that live roots could be extracted and the outer face reinstated on a sound surface. The ends of the walls, being exposed on three sides, tended to have suffered frost damage and many had to be partially rebuilt. To do this imitating the random character of the rubble wall core was surprisingly difficult. Many of the early repairs done a century ago, such as the piers either side of the chapter house entrance, have a smooth face of regular sized flints suggesting that the Abbey was a flint building which, of course, it was not.

The top two metres or so of the walls are the hard capping dating from 1980s. The transept chapel proved to be in good condition with very few loose flints needing re-bedding, however the west and south walls were different. Here the hard flint capping turned out to be loose and friable. There was no alternative to wholesale removal, exposing the original core inside. This was then directly consolidated with a layer of lime mortar. The south face of the transept facing the chapter house had also suffered badly from erosion and needed temporary propping while loose material was removed and replaced with substantial re-facing and a shallow buttress. A weakness was found in the masonry above the previously repaired archway into the adjacent treasury passage (see page 40). A missing masonry pier was reinstated in order to provide additional support.

In the chapter house the hard capping was generally sound, apart from at the very top where the flints were loose. These were removed and the wall tops consolidated with a lime mortar harling mix. Work was required at the point where the remains of the once-vast barrel vault overhang the walls below. Water run-off here was causing erosion and loosening the stones. Deep re-pointing, areas of re-facing and surface consolidation were used to strengthen the walls at this weak point.

Restored chapter house just prior to the re-opening in June 2018.

The south wall of the refectory was added to the project thanks to an additional grant from Historic England. This wall's covering of ivy had to be stripped off before a proper assessment of its condition could be made. The north side, about half of which is masked by the brick wall of a former lean-to green house, was in poor condition with the masonry generally loosened under a tangled mat of ivy roots. Mature ivy roots had to be extracted and loose sections of hard mortar removed to expose the original core of the wall, which was then consolidated. A large recess filled with earth and rubble turned out to be part of an original 'mural' stair. A small area of original internal plaster and a piece of stone window mullion were uncovered. In order to preserve this plaster it has been consolidated, protected and covered back over behind a new screen wall built in front of the recess.

The southern half of the dormitory had a thin and brittle hard capping which was cracking and coming loose. Underneath this, the earthy wall core was soft and friable as a result of extensive root penetration. Some wall height had to be lost in the process of getting down to sound fabric which could be

Re-opening of the Abbey Ruins to the public in June 2018.

consolidated. Surviving plaster fragments within various openings in this wall were identified and targeted for consolidation work.

The tops of all the walls were given a turf soft capping. Following advice from Historic England this was done in a slightly different way to the trials. Turf was cut for it on site to make sure it contained species that thrive naturally in this location and, instead of choosing between grass and sedum, a mixture of both was used, allowing one or other to dominate depending on weather conditions.

ABBEY QUARTER TOUR

Opposite page:
Remnants of flooring tiles retrieved
from the site which is now Forbury Square
are thought to have been used in the paths
within the Abbey kitchen garden. In 2003
images from the tiles were included in
the design of the Forbury Square standing
stone and in a lighting feature of the
landscaped square.

Paper cut design made for carving
the Forbury Square standing stone
by Sally Castle.

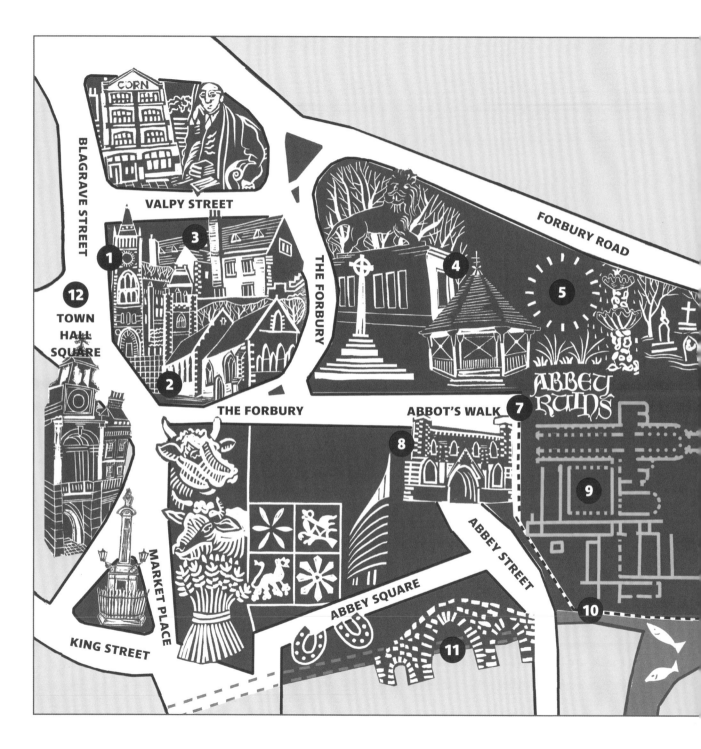

READING ABBEY QUARTER

1. Reading Museum and Art Gallery
2. St Laurence's church, Town Hall Square
3. St Laurence's churchyard and hospitium
4. Forbury Gardens
5. Forbury Hill
6. St James's church
7. Abbots Walk, cloister and refectory
8. Abbey Gateway
9. Abbey Ruins
10. Chestnut Walk
11. Abbey mill arch
12. Town Hall Square

Reading Museum and Art Gallery

Diorama of Reading Abbey wharf on display in Reading Museum.

Opposite page:
Abbey display at Reading Museum

Hallowing of the Church at Reading Abbey by Thomas Becket in 1164, oil on canvas by Stephen Reid, 1920.

Reading Abbey objects on display in the Window Gallery.

Start at Reading Museum in Blagrave Street, where there is a display, complete with a model and a diorama, dedicated to Reading Abbey. The display includes one of the finest collections of Romanesque capitals (tops of columns) and voussoirs (wedges from an arch) in the country, originally from the cloister of Reading Abbey, but discovered during the 20th century in garden settings in Sonning (Holme Court and Borough Marsh) and Shiplake. These include the Coronation of the Virgin capital, one of the earliest discovered workings of this image in Europe.

The Reading Abbey paintings are also on display in the Museum and Town Hall. These were commissioned by Dr Jamieson Hurry in the early years of the 20th century and show scenes of the history of the Abbey, from its foundation in 1121 to the execution of Abbot Hugh Cook Faringdon in 1539.

St Laurence's church, Town Hall Square

Leave the museum and turn left towards Town Hall Square. You will pass the Town Hall building, whose central and southern façades, including the clock tower, were designed by Alfred Waterhouse during the 1870s. On your right is the statue of Queen Victoria, sculpted by George Blackall Simonds.

To the left, on Town Hall Square, stands the church of St Laurence, founded by the Abbey after 1121 as a place of worship for both pilgrims coming to the Abbey and the people of the town. It was enlarged in 1196 and substantially rebuilt in the Perpendicular Gothic style in the 15th and 16th centuries. The west tower was completed in 1458. St Laurence's is no longer a parish church but has an active role as a Church of England mission. It is not open to the public on a regular basis.

On either side of the 15th-century west door are crests: to the right, that of the Abbey, featuring the scallop shell of St James the Great; to the left, that of the town of Reading, which is still the crest of Reading Borough Council.

The north-west corner of the tower still shows the impact of shrapnel from the German bomb, dropped on the south side of Town Hall Square in February 1943, that caused the loss of 41 lives and considerable damage to the tower and the town hall clock tower. It effectively destroyed the offices of Blandy & Blandy in between, and the People's Pantry on the south side of the square. A plaque on the wall of Blandy & Blandy, to the left of the church, records this.

The clocktower of Reading Town Hall and St Laurence's church.

Air raid bomb damage at Town Hall Square, February 1943

St Laurence's churchyard and hospitium

Take the path to the left of the church into the churchyard. Halfway along, stop to view to your left the Hospitium of St John (which accommodated pilgrims and other guests), founded in 1189. What you see is part of the dormitory of the hospitium, where the grammar school was based at the time of the Dissolution, hence its survival. It has been in continued use since then and is currently a day nursery.

Continue along the path and note the out-of-place structure in the churchyard to the right. The inscription on the tablet in front of it explains that "This tracery formed part of the west window of St Laurence's church. It was dislodged during enemy action on 10 February 1943." Shortly before the end of the path, to the right, see the memorial to Henry West, who was killed by a whirlwind at Reading Station on 24 March 1840.

At the eastern end of the path, note the height of the churchyard, which is some three feet (one metre) above the road level here. The churchyard was given to St Laurence's by Mary Tudor in 1556, and its height reflects its intensive use thereafter until the mid-19th century as the burial place of the most populous parish in Reading.

Note also the churchyard wall, restored and rebuilt in places by the council in 2015 to address the impact of tree roots. The wall is predominantly 18th century; the churchyard was enlarged in 1791. Some evidence of its earlier Tudor foundations were found on the southern side of the wall near to St Laurence's church.

The churchyard at the back of St Laurence's church.

Tracery which formed part of the west window of St Laurence's church. The Hospitium of St John is in the background.

Forbury Gardens

The Maiwand Lion
in Forbury Gardens

Opposite page:
Views from Forbury Hill

Descend the steps at the end of the path, taking care when crossing The Forbury, and continue through the gateway into Forbury Gardens. Make your way to view the Maiwand Lion, sculpted by George Blackall Simonds in 1886, which commemorates the war dead of the Afghan Campaign 1879–1880.

Turn back to look towards the obelisk just outside the Victoria Gates, on The Forbury. It is a war memorial to those killed during the two World Wars. The gates include a good, painted representation of the Abbey crest.

Forbury Hill

Climb the mound in the centre of Forbury Gardens. From here there is a good view of what was once the outer, public, precinct of the Abbey. The provenance of the mound is not known for certain, but it certainly existed during the Civil War, when it was an integral part of the siege defences of Reading (1643). Core sampling by the University of Reading Archaeology Department in 2017 has found domestic detritus and tiling from the later Middle Ages, suggesting that the mound was made up in part from demolition rubble, likely to be from the Abbey.

Stand facing the Abbey gateway, due south. Look east (left) to St James's Roman Catholic church. Next to it are its presbytery and its former school, now the Forbury Gardens Day Nursery. Behind the church is Reading Gaol, designed by George Gilbert Scott (1843). You can just see the central tower of the prison beyond the nursery; the Abbey Ruins are visible to its right.

To the left of the Abbey gateway is a new building, Abbots House, opposite which, within Forbury Gardens, stands the Forbury Cross, a monument to King Henry I erected by Dr Hurry in 1909. To the right of the gateway you can see the Crown Court (facade 1861).

There is little left of the great Abbey church that would have dominated the scene in the Middle Ages. It stretched from the south-east corner of Forbury Gardens, roughly where the Henry I monument stands (which was placed at what is believed to be the position of the north end of the west front) to beyond the prison wall visible between the ruins. The crossing, surmounted by a central tower, stood where the Forbury Gardens Day Nursery is now. From here, the north transept reached almost to St James's church; the south transept (whose ruins still stand) extended an equal distance in the opposite direction.

St James's church

The baptismal font in St James's church is formed from a capital of one of the Abbey's cloister pillars.

A view of St James's church from Forbury Hill.

Opposite page:
Fallen blocks from the north transept.

View of the remains of the south transept of the Abbey church from Abbots Walk.

Descend from the mound and turn right to leave Forbury Gardens through the gate on the north side. Once outside the gardens, albeit briefly, walk eastwards along Forbury Road (the IDR) alongside the wall of the gardens. It follows the line of the stone wall that marked the northern boundary of the Abbey precinct. At its eastern end, look into the gardens to see the back of a shelter – more like a grotto – constructed in the 19th century out of stone found on the site, including carved stone from the Abbey.

Turn right into St James's church, designed by Augustus Pugin in the Romanesque style to complement the Abbey Ruins and opened in 1840. Both the north and south aisles are later additions. The church's baptismal font is formed from a capital of one of the Abbey's cloister pillars – the Reading Abbey Stone – dug up during excavations at the time of the church's construction. This intricately decorated limestone capital is the largest remaining carved piece of stonework from the Abbey and the only piece found within the Abbey precinct. St James's church has an interpretation board outside and a history of the Abbey inside.

Abbots Walk, cloister and refectory

Walk south from St James's church, noting the two fallen blocks from the north transept that lie at an angle in front of the presbytery, possibly due to having been blown up during the Civil War. Pass the presbytery and the former school. The flint boundary walls on both sides include carved stones from the Abbey.

At the end of the path, pass through an archway, again made from Abbey stones, and turn left into Abbots Walk. At its eastern end it is closed off with iron railings overlooking the Abbey Ruins. Here you can see the remains of the south transept's two eastern chapels.

This is your first close-up view of the ruins, to which you will return later on this walk.

Turn back and go westwards along Abbots Walk, with the terrace of late Regency town houses on your left (south). From here on you will be walking along the former south aisle of the church, towards its west end. The south aisle was the same width as the roadway.

At the end of the terrace, before the new office block (Abbots House), turn left onto a path leading to a small garden square on the left from where you can view the central parts of the Abbey Ruins, primarily the chapter house and dormitory. The sculpture on the grass, 'Robed Figure' (1988) by Elisabeth Frink, originated as part of a three-piece set of statuary called 'The Dorset Martyrs' (1983/1986) still on display in Dorchester.

This garden square covers the southern part of the Abbey cloister – which extended eastwards under today's Abbots House – and the monks' refectory. The southern wall of the garden is the refectory's south wall.

Abbey gateway

View of the Abbey gateway towards the Crown Court and Forbury Hotel.

Trooper Fred Potts VC, commemorating 'the Hero with the Shovel' of Gallipoli.

Return to Abbots Walk and turn left. Walk alongside Abbots House to the Abbey gateway.

This gateway formed part of the boundary between the parts of the Abbey that were open to the public – on the Forbury Gardens side – and the inner, monastic areas to the south, where the monks lived and worked. It was retained at the Dissolution as the entrance to the royal palace that the Tudors developed out of the abbot's house and other monastic buildings.

During the 18th century the Abbey School for Girls (where the novelist Jane Austen was a pupil in 1785–86) was located in buildings around this site, including the gateway. The gateway suffered a partial collapse during a storm in 1861 and was rebuilt by Sir George Gilbert Scott.

Looking down The Forbury to the west, opposite the Crown Court, you see the statue of Trooper Fred Potts VC, erected in 2015 to commemorate 'the Hero with the Shovel' of Gallipoli.

To the right of the Crown Court is the Forbury Hotel, formerly the Shire Hall of Berkshire County Council (1911).

Abbey Ruins

Henry I memorial

The archway leading into the Abbey Ruins from Forbury Gardens is constructed of carved stones found on site.

Go back into Forbury Gardens through the entrance opposite the Abbey gateway. There is a refreshment kiosk here, with toilets behind. Turn right and follow the line of Abbots Walk inside the Gardens; this will take you past the Henry I memorial. At this point you will be walking along the line of the nave of the Abbey church.

Leave Forbury Gardens through the late 19th-century archway into the Abbey Ruins. The archway is constructed of carved stones found on site. The land on which the arch was built was donated to the corporation by J.J. Wheble and St James's.

The path now takes you into the conserved Abbey Ruins. It follows the eastern aisle of the Abbey cloister. You pass, in order: the south transept, a passageway above which the treasury was located, the chapter house, and the passageway to the infirmary and the monks' dormitory. All are well signed and explained on site.

On the chapter house walls are monuments to commemorate the first and last abbots of the Abbey and the writing-down of the round *Sumer is Icumen in*.

In the grounds of the dormitory, during the Second World War, an air-raid shelter for St James's school was dug. At the southern end of the dormitory was the reredorter – the monks' toilet block. This would have been cleaned by a water channel running off the Holy Brook.

Walk to the end of the path and exit through the gate on to Chestnut Walk.

Chestnut Walk

Oscar Wilde Memorial Walk

'Ball Heads' (2000) by Jens-Flemming Sørensen

Walk down the River Kennet, which is joined by the Holy Brook at this point. This is where the Abbey wharf would have been. To your left, between the river and the perimeter wall of Reading Gaol (where Oscar Wilde was imprisoned from 1895 to 1897), is Chestnut Walk, which features a series of memorials to Wilde: the words 'Oh beautiful world' set into the railings, red love seats, a prison-style bench of the same size as Wilde's prison bed, and the east entrance gates.

To your right is a grassed area with a central sculpture, 'Ball Heads' (2000) by the Danish sculptor Jens-Flemming Sørensen. Beyond it is the outer wall of the monks' refectory.

Abbey mill arch

Abbey Mill arch

Take the path to your right, walk past and around the late 20th-century office block to your left, cross Abbey Street bearing left in front of The Blade (2009), and follow the path next to the Holy Brook on the left of The Blade. Ahead of you is the Abbey mill arch, all that remains of the once-bustling Abbey mill. When the Abbey was in use, the Holy Brook powered the mill and acted as a means of drainage for the Abbey complex. The mill continued in use after the Dissolution up to 1959.

Return to Town Hall Square

At this point you have a choice:

Route 1 (for the intrepid): cross the Holy Brook, walk under the arch and follow the rough path westwards before crossing the Holy Brook again at the back of Reading Central Library, where you can climb the steep steps to reach Abbey Square, the site of the Abbey stables.

Route 2 (for the less adventurous): from the Abbey mill arch, take the steps up into Abbey Square. Turn left and follow Abbey Square past the Abbey Baptist Church to the back of Reading Central Library. Here you will rejoin Route 1.

Continue along and around the library towards the front, where you will see the Holy Brook again as it emerges from a culvert (which it enters just outside The Oracle shopping centre on Gun Street.) The lining of the Holy Brook culvert under the town centre includes carved stones from Reading Abbey.

The Abbey's south gate stood opposite the front entrance to the library, at the junction of Abbey Square and King's Road.

Turn right into Kings Road (a 'new' road dating from the 1830s) and walk westwards to Jackson's Corner. Here you turn right into High Street and approach what was once the Abbey market place. Its triangular shape is a feature of monastic market design. In the centre is the Simeon Monument, a lantern, also triangular, commissioned by Edward Simeon, a Director of the Bank of England, and erected in 1804 to a design by Sir John Soane.

Beyond Market Place are St Laurence's church, Town Hall Square and Reading Museum, where our walk began.

Abbey Square
Town Hall Square

Opposite page:
Market Place Square with Simeon
Monument, linocut by Sally Castle.

Bibliography

Baxter, R., *The Royal Abbey of Reading*. Woodbridge: The Boydell Press, 2016

Hylton, S., *Reading Places, Reading People*. Reading: Berkshire Books, 1992

Hurry, J.B., *Reading Abbey*. London: Elliot Stock, 1901

Kemp, B.R., *Reading Abbey: An introduction to the history of the Abbey*. Reading: Reading Museum and Art Gallery, 1968

Mullaney, J., *Reading's Abbey Quarter: An illustrated history*. Reading: Scallop Shell Press, 2014

Mullaney, J., *The Reading Abbey Stone*. Reading: Scallop Shell Press, 2016

Slade, C. *The Town of Reading and its Abbey*. Reading: Privately published, 2001

More publications can be found in the Reading Library Local Studies Collection, and websites such as www.readingabbeyquarter.org.uk, www.readingmuseum.org.uk, www.readingabbey.org.uk, www.readingabbeyhistory.com.

A list of relevant articles in the *Berkshire Archaeological Journal* can be found in and accessed through The Friends of Reading Abbey website (www.readingabbey.org.uk).

Further reading

Astill, G.G., *Historic Towns in Berkshire: an archaeological appraisal*. Reading: Berkshire Archaeological Trust Ltd, 1978

Coates, A., *English Medieval Books: the Reading Abbey Collection from foundation to dispersal*. Oxford: Oxford Historical Monographs 1999

Coates, C., *The History and Antiquities Of Reading*. London: J Nichols And Son, 1802

Darbyshire, C., *Hugh Cook Faringdon, Last Abbot of Reading*. Reading: Scallop Shell Press, 2018

Dils, J., Reading St Laurence Churchwardens' Accounts 1498–1570 (2 vols), *Berkshire Record Society* Vols. 19 and 20, 2013

Dils, J., *A History of Reading*. Lancaster: Carnegie Publishing, to be published

Escobar-Vargas, M. and Cleaver, L. (eds), Reading Medieval Studies, Vol. XLII *Special Edition on Reading Abbey*. Reading: Graduate Centre for Medieval Studies, University of Reading, 2016

Hurry, J.B., *The Rise and Fall of Reading Abbey*. London, 1906

Hurry, J.B., *Sumer is icumen in*. London, 1914

Kemp (ed.), B.R., *Reading Abbey Cartularies*, Camden Fourth Series, vol 31 (1986) and 33 (1987). London: Royal History Society, 1986/1987

Kemp, B.R., Reading Abbey Records: a new miscellany, *Berkshire Record Society* Vol. 25. Reading, 2018

Man, J., *The history and antiquities, ancient and modern, of the borough of Reading, in the county of Berks*. Reading: Snare and Man, 1816

Mullaney, J., *Reformation, Revolution and Rebirth*. Reading: Scallop Shell Press, 2012

Publisher's acknowledgements and picture credits

The publishers are grateful to a number of people and organisations for permission to reproduce photos and paintings in this book: Reading Museum (Reading Borough Council), the British Library, Reading Library and Berkshire Record Office for the historic paintings and photographs; Chris Forsey, Joanne Spice, Nadja Guggi, Anne Nolan, Ron Baxter, David Illif, John Mullaney and Frances Stradling for the photographs; Sally Castle for her linocuts and John R. Mullaney for his picture of the Abbey. In particular, we would like to thank Jess Freeland at Reading Museum for her diligent detective work, and Katie Amos at Reading Library and Margaret Dinham at Berkshire Record Office for their friendly and efficient support. We are grateful to the Earley Charity for again funding one of our publications. Without them, there would be fewer good books about Reading!

p. x Illustration by John R. Mullaney. FSAI (www.thetopdraw.com)

p. 2 Henry I window. © Nadja Guggi

p. 3 Abbey model. © Reading Borough Council (Reading Museum)

p. 4 Englefield plan. © Reading Borough Council (Reading Museum)

p. 5 Hurry plan. Courtesy of the illustrations collection, Reading Central Library

p. 6 Henry I. © The British Library Board. Royal 14 C.VII, f.8v

p. 7 Linocut. © Sally Castle
Henry I memorial plaque. © Nadja Guggi

p. 8 OS map. © Reading Borough Council (Reading Museum)
Cholsey Barn. Courtesy of the illustrations collection, Reading Central Library

p. 9 Thomas Becket. © Nadja Guggi

p. 10 'Sumer Is Icumen In'. © Reading Borough Council (Reading Museum)

p. 12 Hugh of Amiens memorial. © Joanne Spice

p. 13 Election of the Mayor. © Reading Borough Council (Reading Museum)

p. 14 Monks reading. © Reading Borough Council (Reading Museum)
Cellarer. © The British Library Board. Sloane 2435, f.44v

p. 15 Hugh Faringdon. © Nadja Guggi

p. 16 Abbey's emblem. © Nadja Guggi
Head of pilgrim. © Chris Forsey

p. 17 Hand of St James. © Ron Baxter

p. 19 Speed map. © Reading Borough Council (Reading Museum)

p. 21 1254 agreement. © Berkshire Record Office (R/IC3/1)

p. 22 Marriage at the Abbey. © Reading Borough Council (Reading Museum)

p. 25 Edward IV presents Elizabeth. © Reading Borough Council (Reading Museum)

p. 26 Parliament. © Reading Borough Council (Reading Museum)

p. 28 Burial of Henry I. © Reading Borough Council (Reading Museum)

p. 30 Digital 3D reconstruction. © Reading Borough Council (Reading Museum)

p. 32 Abingdon gateway. © Frances Stradling

p. 33 Digital 3D reconstruction. © Reading Borough Council (Reading Museum)

p. 34 South transept. © Nadja Guggi

p. 35 Peterborough Cathedral. Photo by David Iliff. License: CC-BY-SA 3.0

p. 36 Tile floor. © Reading Borough Council (Reading Museum)

p. 37 Digital 3D reconstruction. © Reading Borough Council (Reading Museum)

p. 38 Cloister reconstruction. © Reading Borough Council (Reading Museum)

p. 94 & 95   All three re-opening pictures. © Chris Forsey

p. 96   Paper cut design. © Sally Castle

p. 98 & 99   Abbey Quarter Map. © Sally Castle

p. 100   Consecration of the Abbey. © Reading Borough
Council (Reading Museum)
Reading Museum display © Reading Borough Council
(Reading Museum)
Reading Museum objects. © Nadja Guggi

p. 101   Diorama. © Reading Borough Council
(Reading Museum)

p. 102   St Laurence's. © Nadja Guggi
Bomb damage. Chronicle collection.
© Reading Borough Council (Reading Museum)

p. 103   St Laurence's churchyard. © Nadja Guggi

p. 104 & 105   Maiwand Lion and views from Forbury Hill.
© Anne Nolan

p. 106   St James's and the font. © Nadja Guggi

p. 107   Fallen blocks. © Anne Nolan
Abbots Walk. © Nadja Guggi

p. 108   Abbey gateway. © Anne Nolan
Trooper Potts. © Nadja Guggi

p. 109   Memorial cross & Abbey stones. © Anne Nolan

p. 110   Chestnut Walk & Sculpture. © Nadja Guggi

p. 111   Mill arch. © Nadja Guggi

p. 112   Linocut. © Sally Castle

p. 113   Abbey Square and Town Hall Square. © Anne Nolan

The conservation work carried out during 2017 and 2018 involved a huge team and we'd particularly like to give credit to those below:

Reading Borough Council: Matthew Williams, Director Reading Museum; Christelle Beaupoux, Project Manager; Andy Lockwood, Construction Project Manager.

Reading Hampshire Property Partnership: Giles Pritchard, Design Manager & Conservation Architect; Barnaby Wheeler, Project Architect.

Main Contractor: CRL Restoration Ltd; Ben Lawson, contract manager; Roberto Mulé, site manager.

Masonry Contractor: Cliveden Conservation Ltd; Lewis Proudfoot, contract manager; William Skinner, heritage conservator and site manager.

Two Rivers Press has been publishing in and about Reading since 1994.
Founded by the artist Peter Hay (1951–2003), the press continues
to delight readers, local and further afield, with its varied list
of individually designed, thought-provoking books.